Extreme Teaching

Keen J. Babbage

A SCARECROWEDUCATION BOOK

The Scarecrow Press, Inc.
Lanham, Maryland, and Oxford
2002

A SCARECROWEDUCATION BOOK

Published in the United States of America
by Scarecrow Press, Inc.
A Member of the Rowman & Littlefield Publishing Group
4720 Boston Way, Lanham, Maryland 20706
www.scarecroweducation.com

PO Box 317
Oxford
OX2 9RU, UK

British Library Cataloguing in Publication Information Available

Library of Congress Cataloging-in-Publication Data

Babbage, Keen J.
    Extreme teaching / Keen J. Babbage.
        p. cm.
"A ScarecrowEducation book."
Includes index.
    ISBN 0-8108-4350-1 (cloth : alk. paper) — ISBN 0-8108-4349-8 (pbk. :
alk. paper)
    1.Teaching. I. Title.
    LB1025.3 .B33 2002
    371.102—dc21

                                                    2002004982

⊗™ The paper used in this publication meets the minimum requirements of
American National Standard for Information Sciences—Permanence of
Paper for Printed Library Materials, ANSI/NISO Z39.48-1992.
Manufactured in the United States of America.

3

Dedicated to Robert, Julie and Brian

Contents

Preface

"Would you like to teach a critical thinking class to 7th graders?" The question came to me from the principal of the middle school where I was the assistant principal. The question struck me with the same force as if I were asked, "Would you like for your heart to keep beating, your lungs to keep breathing and your brain to keep functioning?" The answer is yes. To have proper functions of my heart, lungs and brain is vital to my life. To teach is also vital to my life.

As a high school sophomore I watched my world civilization teacher one day as she very capably did her work. The thought that vividly emerged in my mind with such power and certainty that it is with me still was, "Keen, you could do that work. You should do that work." From that moment forward I have never doubted that teaching is not merely what I do; teaching is who I am. Despite irresistible adventures with three outstanding companies and despite some equally irresistible adventures as a school administrator, it is teaching in a classroom with students that pumps the blood through my heart, the air through my lungs, the ideas and thoughts through my brain and the purpose into my life. My first name is Keen, which means sharp or clever. With just a bit of poetic license and imagination, the definition of Keen means that my name is almost a synonym for "teacher."

The 7th grade critical thinking students did magnificent work. They reflected, thought, created, invented, analyzed, compared, contrasted, probed, explained, reasoned, learned and succeeded. The average grade was 93. The classroom behavior was exemplary. The students actually asked for more work. "When will we get to do another project?" "Yeah,

Dr. Babbage, when can we do that?" Other students asked how they could get into the class. I was pleased and encouraged, but not satisfied. One characteristic of effective teachers is to never be satisfied.

My first love in education was teaching high school. Opportunities to work in middle schools had been productive and beneficial, but I longed for a reunion with my first love, so I volunteered to work on some committees and some projects that addressed high school topics. I saw some similarities in middle school and high school goals, yet the age differences in the students are major factors in fine-tuning exactly what works best for 6th through 12th graders.

As teaching critical thinking to 7th graders combined with high school committee work, the next steps became clear. First, write a book about teaching so other teachers and their students can benefit from the experiences, adventures, learning and ideas I have journeyed through. Second, teach again full time. The book is being written now. The next teaching adventure is, I hope, imminent.

This book is written both for the reader and for the author. I need to think through the concept of and the implementation of Extreme Teaching so my students and I can have the most extremely amazing learning adventures possible. It is my hope that every reader and his or her students will benefit from this book as you create and experience the energy and impact of Extreme Teaching.

Keen Babbage
Lexington, Kentucky
September 2001

Introduction

"The purpose of a school is to cause learning." In three previous books, I have preached the sermons of school purpose and causing learning. School purpose is deeper than goals for the current school year. School purpose is more fundamental than a mission statement. Goals and missions can change. School purpose is the reason for being, the reason a school exists at all. The purpose of a school is to cause learning.

The verb *cause* is controversial. Some options that are less controversial could include "the purpose of a school is to enable learning" or "to encourage learning" or "to facilitate learning" or "to enhance and foster learning." Those options use words that are lovely, healthy, wholesome and common. Those words are also weak. *Cause* means to make it happen, to get the desired result. Teachers should resent being put in a category of people who are asked merely to enhance, foster, facilitate or encourage learning. Teachers cause learning. The result of real teaching is that learning happens, learning is caused. If teaching occurs, learning happens. If learning does not happen, teaching did not happen. There may have been much work, much activity, many books, lots of homework, several tests, ample use of technology, and many busy people involved in doing much in a classroom at school; however, if all of that busy-ness did not result in learning, we cannot call that process teaching.

"I taught them, but they did not learn" is an inherent contradiction. Efforts were made. Lessons were prepared. Materials were gathered. Activity was evident. Efforts, lessons, materials and activity may be part of what causes learning, but efforts, lessons, materials and activity could be used without learning occurring.

Extreme teaching accepts the premise, the challenge and the standard that the purpose of a school is to cause learning; therefore, the duty of a teacher is to cause learning.

There emerges now an essential question, which has intrigued me in recent years since I began preaching the sermon about the purpose of a school being to cause learning. The next question is, "What is the purpose of learning?"

First, consider this question of the purpose of learning from the perspective of a student who is in middle school or in high school. Jared, a 16-year-old high school sophomore, will give his perspective. "School is, well, you know, it's school. The purpose must be to give students something to do until we're old enough for something real. You go to each class, do the assignments and move on. Most classes are pretty much alike. You get a textbook, you get worksheets, you take tests, you write papers or do projects, you memorize or cram so you can get a good grade or a good enough grade. Once in a while there's a really cool teacher who makes the class fun, but usually classes are pretty dull. I really like soccer and I'm in a computer club where we get to fix anything at school that goes wrong with computers. I have a lot of friends and seeing them is fun. But, you know, there's not much at school that interests me. I wish I could graduate soon, but I have two more years of this to go. What's the purpose of two more years of the same old stuff?"

Second, let's hear from a teacher to get another perspective on the purpose of learning. "I've taught high school for twenty-three years. My students have to leave my class knowing the processes and procedures of algebra and geometry. We complete the material in the textbook every year and I take pride in that. My students are ready to move on to more math in high school or college. That's the purpose of their learning: to be ready for the next level of math."

Third, some words from a parent about the purpose of learning should be added. "I want what's best for my child. I want her to learn all she can and to enjoy doing that. I encourage her to do her best in each class. She needs to earn scholarships for college so she'll have good opportunities. I'd say the purpose of her learning now is for college and career, of course, I also want her to have a good family of her own so that's part of it too."

Is there any common ground in these three perspectives? Is the purpose of learning at school limited to passing a class, making a good grade, preparing for more classes, qualifying for college, training for a job or being ready to lead a family? School learning seems to be related to classroom activities which prepare a student for more classroom activities, which eventually accumulate into a sufficient amount of time, activities and accomplishment that the student is declared to be a high school graduate who can move on to more classroom activities, career duties and/or family commitments.

With a few minor adjustments, I would suggest that the experience of learning at school can be more meaningful, worthwhile, real, fascinating, compelling, useful, practical and inspiring than is common. The purpose of a school is to cause learning. The purpose of learning is to acquire wisdom. The purpose of wisdom is to live well right now and throughout a lifetime. How can learning at school cause wisdom? Wisdom is an extreme degree of learning, so extreme teaching is needed. How does extreme teaching work? Answering that question is the purpose of this book.

The intellectual foundation for this book comes from research, reflection, and experience. The research was done originally for my 1998 book *High-Impact Teaching: Overcoming Student Apathy*. When asked to indicate what their best teachers had done in the classroom that caused learning, the research participants provided insights that emphasized four essential and effective aspects of their great teachers:

1. They challenged students and they challenged themselves.
2. They used a variety of teaching methods with emphasis on active involvement of students.
3. They were enthusiastic and encouraging.
4. They connected learning with students' lives now, in their real worlds.

Since the publication of that book, I have repeatedly sought to improve, confirm or correct that research. Whenever I speak to educators, to students, or to civic groups I ask this question: "What did the best teacher you ever had do that made the classroom experience so great, so memorable, so beneficial to you?" People smile as they recall the experiences in that classroom. People eagerly give their answers.

The replies have always confirmed the original research. There are no secrets to great teaching. We know what works. Great teachers have mastered the four elements in *High-Impact Teaching* listed above.

I reflect on teaching often. As an elementary, middle school, high school, college, and graduate student I often critiqued my teachers silently. I noted what worked and promised myself I would borrow those methods. I resented classroom experiences that were unproductive, ordinary, mundane and superficial. In those classes I would wonder how the class should have been taught. I now ask students about school. Their insight ignites much reflection. I observe colleagues teaching and think of ideas I can share to help them reach their goals with students. All of those reflections will be incorporated into this book.

The intellectual foundation for this book will include experiences I have had in the classroom during the past 21 years as an educator, with special attention to recent experiences because in those adventures I tried the methods of Extreme Teaching and found the response from and the results for students to surpass all expectations.

As a college student, I took two classes in economics. Two economic concepts that especially intrigued me were opportunity costs and elastic/inelastic products. On two separate occasions in the 7th grade critical thinking classes I taught, I heard students give answers that absolutely amazed me: "Because salt is inelastic" and "That is due to the opportunity costs." In both cases, I enthusiastically acknowledged the profound answers. I also told the students that at age 13 they knew what it took me until age 19 to learn. They found great satisfaction in being six years ahead of their teacher. With the possibility of such extreme learning within our reach, our imagination, our teaching, and our students each moment of each day, anything less than extreme teaching is unacceptable.

This book is written for teachers. An increasing number of teachers are frustrated and disappointed because a growing number of students do not take schoolwork seriously and do not make much effort to learn at school. This book is designed to help give teachers some ideas, some actions, some methods, some lessons and some lesson design concepts that can help inspire commitment from students.

This book is written for students. An increasing number of students are frustrated and disappointed because a growing number of classes they take and textbooks they read just do not seem worth much time and effort. For too many students, the classroom experience at school gets a one-word evaluation: "boring." This book is designed to help give teachers and their students some perspectives and some activities that can energize a classroom with purpose, fascination, commitment and learning.

This book is written for school administrators, school board members, and political leaders. These determined people continually seek an effective reform of education that will work better than prior reforms. They can save time by realizing that the reform that matters more than all other reforms is great teaching, effective teaching, teaching that causes learning; what this book calls Extreme Teaching.

This book is written for parents and guardians who seek ways to create meaningful learning experiences for their children and teenagers in the daily interactions of family life. The teaching methods in this book can be adapted to lessons that families need to teach at home.

Please note, all of my experience in teaching and in school administration has been with middle school, high school, college and graduate school. The ideas in this book are designed with grades 6–12 in mind; however, those ideas can, I trust, be used by elementary school teachers and by college professors, with adjustments made as needed.

It will please me when readers of this book implement the ideas and the methods of Extreme Teaching in ways that improve teaching and learning. It will please me more when readers build upon, expand, and add to the ideas and methods of Extreme Teaching due to this book stimulating readers to think anew, to create and to be invigorated. Toward this end, let's begin our stimulating adventure of Extreme Teaching.

CHAPTER 1

Reality

"You know, Ms. Armstrong, that worksheet we did in your social studies class on chapter 12 when I was a junior in high school really changed my life."

That statement will never be made because worksheets do not change lives, and chapter 12 in any high school textbook does not change lives.

"Mr. Prather, you remember one day in your 9th-grade consumer math class we debated whether information in television commercials was true or not? My job was to defend the company that had the commercial. Some other students represented consumer groups and government agencies. Well, I'm a senior in college now. I'm already accepted to attend a great law school next year. I want to specialize in corporate law. It all started in your class and continued when you got me to join the debate team you coached. I just, you know, wanted to say thanks, Mr. Prather. You really made a difference in my life."

Great teachers know how to cause learning. What great teachers know is available to anyone: just ask a great teacher for ideas, seek the guidance of a great teacher, knock on the classroom door of a great teacher and ask, "May I watch you teach, please, and learn from your example?"

We know what works. Let's repeat those words, please: *We know what works.* Socrates did not keep his teaching method to himself. Any teacher can borrow the Socratic method. Read Plato's "Meno" and do what Socrates does in that essay, case study, and interactive teaching episode. Current teachers whose students learn, become inspired, reach new goals, think new thoughts and dream new dreams share their methods, motivations and work ethic via articles in professional journals, books, conferences, workshops, professional development sessions, websites, videos and personal conversations.

We know what works. We also know what does not work. Imagine a classroom where a new chapter in the old textbook is begun each Monday and the following sequence is used every week:

Monday:	Read the chapter. Make a list of all words in bold print. Write the meaning of each bold print word.
Tuesday:	Write an outline of the chapter using the headings and subheadings as key topics.
Wednesday:	Complete three worksheets that were provided by the textbook publisher.
Thursday:	Take a quiz on the chapter.
Friday:	Take a test on the chapter.

That classroom is in a coma and on life support. Ten years after high school, can any student remember any chapter from any school textbook? Contrast that question with this inquiry: how many students can remember great teachers and the vibrant experiences they had in the classrooms of those great teachers, even though 10 or more years have passed since high school graduation? Textbooks and worksheets are forgotten. Energetic interaction and meaningful learning experiences in vibrant classrooms are remembered because they are real, worthwhile, meaningful and important when they happen and they provide reality, worth, meaning and importance in the future and for the future.

We know what works. We know what great teachers do. We also know what great students do. I asked 7th graders what is required to learn and succeed at school. The answers were given instantly, accurately, and confidently. "Do your work." "Pay attention in class to the teacher." "Turn in homework." "Turn in all of your homework on time." "Stay out of trouble." "Take notes." "Don't lose your work." "Be on time." "Bring your stuff to class." "Listen." "Follow the rules." "Follow instructions." "Don't cheat." "Don't goof off." "Don't act silly or bother people." "Study." The answers came easily, but putting those answers into action is the challenge. Saying the words is easy, but implementing the ideas and the actions conveyed by the words is the larger duty.

With these thoughts in mind, let's hear a conversation between a school district superintendent and the district's assistant superintendent for curriculum and instruction. The topic of discussion is test scores. The schools in the district just are not progressing sufficiently on the annual assessment tests that are required by the state department of education. Superintendent Edward Adams and Assistant Superintendent Paula Hammisch have reviewed the most recent test scores and are wondering what to do.

Adams: This is awful. We're going nowhere unless we're going backward or downhill. One or two schools show some progress, but six of the elementary schools and two of the middle schools were even with or below last year's scores, and one high school showed some minor gains while the other high school reversed three straight years of improvement and dropped its score. What's the explanation and what needs to be done? I know it's not easy or simple, but we've tried every possible education reform. We follow every new law. We've had endless training and professional development for faculty and staff. What's your perspective on all this? I'm about to conclude that we've done all we can do.

Hammisch: I wish I knew the perfect solution. We *have* tried every possible innovation. We *do* follow every law and regulation. We do what the state tells us to do. We attend all of the right conferences and workshops. We train our people every year in new ideas. We have invested in technology and reading programs and violence prevention programs and everything else that looked like it could help. My best advice is that we get fresh input from teachers and students. Let's see what they think, since they're where the action is in school. We could get input from parents, guardians and other citizens, too, but the people who are in school each day are best informed. I could set up a group of teachers and a group of students to begin the process.

Adams: OK, let's move as quickly as possible. Let's avoid being bureaucratic, though; the school board and the community will not be pleased when these test scores show up in the newspaper in a few days, and they won't settle for a bunch of committee meetings as a real solution. Check with the principals and with the president of the teachers' group in the district and get four names of teachers to include from middle schools and high schools. Let's have you meet with them first.

You know, we started a similar group last year with elementary schools. Get that elementary group's report out and add any updates that are necessary because of these new test scores. Also, get some middle school and high school students to meet with you, maybe at a school or a pizza place. See what they're thinking. Sometimes we can learn a lot from students instead of paying for experts to visit us and tell us what we need. The same is true with teachers. Let's get some real insights from them about what's good and bad in our schools and what needs to be done.

Hammisch: Dr. Adams, here's one other idea. Let's promise ourselves and our colleagues and our students and our community that we're going to solve this problem. When the test scores are made public, let's offer no excuse or rationalization. Let's just say that we will do what it takes for all students to learn and for all students to succeed. Let's tell the community we're going to look deeply into our district to see what's working and what's not working; to trade our best ideas with each other and replace ideas that aren't working. Let's assure them that we want to move quickly, but sensibly.

Adams: Good thinking. That will be our attitude and our message. Update me often and involve me whenever I can be helpful. Thanks, Paula.

Paula Hammisch had been a great middle school social studies teacher for seven years. She had then taught high school social studies for 10 years and won state and national teaching awards. She accepted the job of assistant superintendent for curriculum and instruction on the condition that she would be allowed to continue teaching one middle school class or one high school class each year. Dr. Adams had eagerly agreed with her request because students would have a great teacher, because teachers would know that Paula did the same kind of work they did instead of just staying in an office away from the schools, because Paula loved to teach and because the entire school district needed to benefit from Paula's expertise, talent, enthusiasm, skill and wisdom.

Paula had worked with a group of elementary teachers last year because those teachers and their principals had seen problems emerging

and increasing in number and complexity: from more children on med-
ication to controlling severe misbehaviors to more children being
reared by grandparents, aunts, uncles or foster families; from more
children entering school with very little at-home reading experience to
more children getting disruptive or violent at school. Most elementary
students were behaving and learning reasonably, but the number of personal family, medical, psychological, learning disability or court involvement problems surfacing in the elementary schools had been increasing so much that, every day, some severe situation could occur.
Problems that once had been associated with middle school students or
high school students were now clearly part of elementary school reality. The Lakewood school district's task force—called the Lakewood
Elementary Achievement Results Needed (L.E.A.R.N.) committee—
had created some recommendations for student achievement, school
safety, test scores, family involvement at school, and school-family
communication and had completed a report for the board of education
to consider at an upcoming meeting. An equally thorough effort was
now needed for middle schools and high schools.

Who should be part of the teacher committee that Ms. Hammisch
would form? Only the best teachers in the district? Only very experienced teachers? A demographically diverse group to perfectly represent
all cultures, backgrounds, ethnicity, age groups, genders and values?
All of that seemed to be excessively contrived. Instead, Paula spoke
with principals and was given names of teachers who do their job of
teaching in very different ways. Ms. Hammisch had long ago concluded that of all the variables that impact learning at school and that
can be controlled by the adults at a school, the effectiveness of teaching was more important than anything else; in truth, it was more important than everything else. Paula did not seek the most popular teachers or the most respected teachers. She sought a variety of teachers
based on how they taught and on how they thought about teaching.
From that realistic range of teaching methods and teaching attitudes,
perspectives, ideas and concepts, some deep understanding and some
revealing insights about what students experience at school and why
that experience is getting the current less-than-acceptable results could
emerge. Let's meet the teachers Paula Hammisch would invite to gather
for an initial, informal discussion.

Jason Prather loves to teach. Students love to be in Mr. Prather's classes. Whether you are a high school student who thinks that math is fascinating or one who thinks that math is a curse, you love being in Mr. Prather's math classes. You work, you learn, you get inspired, and you actually enjoy it. Mr. Prather does not design his classes to be fun. He designs them to be fascinating. High school math students who are fascinated by math and by their math teacher's creative ways of teaching will say "class was fun" when the educational jargon might have been "math class today stimulated me to use higher-order thinking skills as we measured, analyzed, predicted, evaluated, probed and reasoned using math concepts and cognitive abilities." Mr. Prather loves to teach because he loves to be with students, he loves math and he loves the adventures that can occur in a classroom where teacher, students and math energetically, creatively and purposefully interact daily.

With 13 years of teaching experience, Mr. Prather almost never thinks of retirement. By the numbers, he could retire in another 15 years or so, but at that time he will be 50 years old and he expects to have the health and the dedication to take him through many more years of great teaching. Mr. Prather does not count the years until retirement or the days until the next summer vacation. He counts how many students learned everything they needed to learn in math class today, and he creates ideas to take those students further and to help the other students learn better tomorrow.

Mr. Prather had some difficult years earlier in his teaching career. After about five years of teaching, he seriously thought of taking his math skills to a computer company or to a life insurance company. He had interviews with several companies, and he had two very attractive job offers. The income, at least the part measured in dollars, would have been more than he makes as a teacher. The companies even offered some stock purchase plans and other lucrative benefits. But when Mr. Prather searched his heart and his soul and his mind, he confidently decided to stay in teaching. There was one reason: At every company where he interviewed, there were no high school students. There was plenty of math work to do. There were plenty of job challenges. There were plenty of opportunities for career advancement. Those are important aspects of corporate careers and Mr. Prather was intrigued by those opportunities, but he realized that the work he loves is teaching math to high school students. Using his math skill was not the most important part of his job; using his math skill and his teaching skill to cause high school students to learn math and to be fascinated with math, those results are what matter most to Mr. Prather.

There have been a few other frustrations for Mr. Prather in his teaching career. He can get frustrated when school district officials or school principals get excited about a new fad that everyone has to learn and use but that in a year will be replaced with another new fad. Mr. Prather is always willing to use better ideas and better teaching methods, but he has seen some innovations imposed on teaching that he thought someone should have realized were just not going to work. Mr. Prather's heart breaks whenever a high school student drops out of school.

He knows that some of these factors just have to be accepted as the current reality, but one person at a time, one student at a time, he will touch the lives he can reach from his position as a classroom teacher. There are frustrations with any job, Mr. Prather has decided, but there are some accomplishments that can happen only in a high school classroom. If you are going to touch the lives of students, you have to be where the students are. For Mr. Prather, that means to be in the high school math classroom showing students how much more they already know about math than they realized and how much more they can learn. He will also show them that math is pretty neat, cool, fascinating and, as every student hopes school will be, fun. Mr. Prather does not set out to make math fun, but fun is a by-product of math being real, useful, practical, meaningful, worthwhile, fascinating and challenging. Mr. Prather is the teacher every student hopes to get for math and the teacher every parent or guardian hopes his or her child gets for math. Still, he will tell you that he tries each year to improve, to grow, to do better as a teacher. He sees himself as a good teacher, but he seeks to be a great teacher. He is much closer to greatness than he admits. The best teachers are like that. They do not realize how good they are because they expect to always become better and better.

Ms. Angela Overstreet has been a middle school science teacher for 22 years. Twenty-three years ago when Ms. Overstreet was a college senior, a professor told everyone in her teaching methods class that use of an overhead projector was the state of the art in teaching. Using the overhead projector was superior to using a chalkboard or a textbook, the professor said. Put it on the overhead projector, show it on a screen so every student can see, use several colors of marker pens so the emphasis can be made in living color and the students will learn, learn and learn. It did not take long for Ms. Overstreet to be nicknamed—by the teachers, not by the students—Ms. Overhead.

All day, every day for the past 22 years, Ms. Overstreet has begun the day by turning on the overhead projector and ended the day by turning off the overhead projector. No students have ever been turned on to science in Ms. Overstreet's class as much as the overhead projector has been. Ms. Overstreet does not talk to the students very much. She does not look at the students very much. She does not interact with the students very much. But she talks to, she looks at and she interacts with the overhead projector a lot. She is doing what, as she understands, her college professor told her she was supposed to do. Nothing she is doing is against current school district policies. She has been told to use other teaching methods and other teaching tools, but whenever an administrator challenges her methods, Ms. Overstreet brings in a representative from her teacher association and the confrontation begins. Administrators who have continued to challenge Ms. Overstreet have found that it took so much time that their other duties suffered. So Ms. Overstreet and the overhead projector continue to have a great time together, and students obediently copy whatever is written on the overhead.

Students do not ask questions in class very often. Students do not answer questions in class very often either, because usually when Ms. Overstreet asks a question, she answers it herself and writes both the question and the answer on the overhead projector. It should be easy to make an A in this class, but few students do, even though it is very clear what must be done: write and memorize what is written on the overhead projector sheets. Most of the students hate the class. Many of the students rarely do the homework or study for tests. These students protest in the only way they can: by silently refusing to do anything beyond what is necessary to pass the class. Sure, some students comply, and they make good grades. They cannot afford to make low grades because they would get in trouble at home or because it would impact their grade point averages. Still, each day is an ordeal for the students to endure in Ms. Overstreet's classroom.

The amazing aspects of Ms. Overstreet are that she arrives very early for school and she stays very late. It has taken time to prepare the overhead transparency sheets she uses day after day, year after year. New textbooks every six years require new transparency sheets for the old overhead projector. She prides herself on having precisely arranged overhead transparencies for all of the chapters in the science book. If it is the tenth week of the school year, she is using transparencies 10a, 10b, 10c, 10d and 10e. There is at least one transparency for each day of the week. She uses a few other materials that the textbook publisher provides. She even creates some transparencies on her own. She has the most complete and the best organized collection of middle school science transparencies for overhead projectors anyone can imagine. But so what? Science is not learned very deeply or very eagerly in Ms. Overstreet's classroom. Overhead transparencies do not teach much science to anyone. A few science terms are memorized by conscientious students who copy the words and store the words in their memories until the test is over, but then the words are forgotten.

Ms. Overstreet is very polite and friendly. She willingly accepts duties such as helping supervise at a football or basketball game. She volunteers to help the committee that organizes the annual September open house evening at school. She turns her grades in on time. She has a very good attendance record at school. Plus, what she does in the classroom is allowed and she can defend it. And she has avoided being unprofessional. One principal told her that each day in each class she had to use two teaching methods that did not involve the overhead projector. On the next day she used part of a video about earthquakes and part of another video about space exploration. From overhead projector to video player was not the dramatic, fascinating, interactive, challenging and meaningful teaching method the principal had had in mind, but Ms. Overstreet had complied with the request. Few administrators make requests of Ms. Overstreet now, because the result is so limited or so frustrating; she is obedient to the letter of the requests but not to the spirit and real intent of the requests.

The best insight about Ms. Overstreet came from one student who said, "I wish she paid as much attention to us as she does the overhead projector. What's so neat about that machine?" The answer is, nothing. The machine is what Ms. Overstreet was told to use when she was a college senior 23 years ago. She is doing what she was told to do when she was preparing to teach. That is what got her through her college classes, through her teacher preparation program, through her teaching certification requirements and through her first few years of teaching, so it is what she continues to do out of habit, out of loyalty, and out of the assumption, "What was good enough for my professor to tell me must still be good enough for my students to experience today." Did the students learn or not? That is not the question to Ms. Overstreet. Did I show them what they are supposed to learn? and Did I give them the chance to learn? Those are the questions Ms. Overstreet asks herself, and the answer she always gives to herself is yes. Because of that, Ms. Overstreet thinks that she is a good teacher. She is a well-organized classroom clerk, but what she does in the classroom is not teaching.

Katie Fletcher has taught high school French for three years. She is a great teacher, but she would quit today if a better job came along. She does not expect the better job, but she continues to look. What makes Katie so good in the classroom? She mastered French when she was in high school. She majored in French in college and spent her junior year of college in Paris. She thinks in French. She says that her dreams are in French. She is totally fascinated with the French language, the French culture, the history of France, the people of France, and every-thing else French. Her students usually fit into one of two categories: the students who catch and match Ms. Fletcher's dedication to every-thing French, and the students who cannot see any reason to learn French because they will never go to France, or have a job where French is spoken. These students in the second category do little work for a class that does not have a very practical application right now.

It would be great if Ms. Fletcher could find enough career satisfac-tion from the students who do respond, and if she could use that inspi-ration to find ways to motivate the other students. Instead, Ms. Fletcher just prefers to move on to another job at the first possible opportunity. If the other students would show any interest, show any appreciation, make any effort in French class, maybe it would be worth it, but that has not happened. Because French fascinated Ms. Fletcher in high school and in college, she figured that high school students would ap-preciate the opportunity to learn it and that their parents or guardians

would want them to learn it. She notices that the students who make little or no effort in her class seem to make little or no effort in most of
their other classes as well. What does this generation of students expect?
she wonders. Ms. Fletcher is not that much older than the students, and
she worked hard in school and did well in her classes. Sure, she loved
French and it came easy to her, but she also worked very hard in other
classes that she found difficult and less enjoyable. Have students
changed so much in just 5 or 10 years that many of them cannot be
taught no matter what a teacher does? Teaching just has not worked out
the way she planned, so she is willing to change her plans and move on.

Ken Belton will teach for the rest of his life. He will coach a sport
each year for the rest of his life. He will sponsor a student organization each year for the rest of his life. Ken has taught for 19 years and
is perfectly content. He teaches physical education and also some
health classes. Before teaching, Ken worked for seven years in state
government by day and attended college by night. At age 25, his
dream came true and he began teaching. Ken is a good guy, liked by
his colleagues. Ken's physical education students are typical of most
middle school students: some really like sports and games, some like
a few sports and games and others dislike any physical activity because they are not good at sports or games or because getting hot and
dirty in gym class makes them look less cool and stylish the rest of
the day.

If you checked the grades of Ken's students you would see a rather
ordinary, predictable distribution of grades: a few As, some Bs, a lot of
Cs, some Ds and a few Fs. Ken tries to motivate the students who do
poorly, and once in a long while a student will respond. Ken's classes
are orderly and his students behave well. Ken's students leave the class
with pretty much the same attitude they brought—if it was good, it
stayed good; if it was bad, it stayed bad. Ken wishes that more students
did better, but he really gives it a good effort. He has tried some new
methods, has gone to some new training sessions for teachers, checks
with other teachers to see what they are doing. Ken makes some phone
calls to the parents or guardians of students who are doing poorly.
Sometimes the student in question will do better for a few days, and
other times there is no noticeable difference at all. But at least Ken tries.

At the end of each school year, Ken leaves for three months and returns in August to try it all again. The principal of the school can rely on Ken to be there, to be conscientious, to be on time, to be on duty and to be professional. Ken is a typical teacher.

His principal would like for him to be a great teacher and would like for all of the Kens in the school to be great teachers. The principal is convinced that Ken would like to be great and that other teachers would like to be great. Schools are places where hope is alive; the challenge is to implement that hope so all teachers and all students succeed.

Paula Hammisch sees herself as a keeper of hope, and she sees her new assignment from the superintendent as a way to put hope into effective action.

Paula also knows that for any teaching reform to be truly effective, it must be implemented fully and it must be implemented well by every teacher in every classroom of every school or the results will suffer and the innovation could fail. Failure would not be because it was a bad idea, but because too few teachers implemented the reform completely and correctly. The Lakewood school district has great, good, average, tolerable and unacceptable teachers, and all of those teachers would have to successfully implement any new teaching reform. The teachers on the committee Paula was organizing could not be from only the superstar select group. Instead, the committee would have a variety of teachers who worked at different levels of quality and of competence, because that is reality and because that helps identify barriers to implementing great innovations.

Paula Hammisch e-mailed Jason Prather, Angela Overstreet, Katie Fletcher and Ken Belton, asking for their participation in a district "think group" to explore ideas for how to improve the quantity and quality of learning by all middle school and high school students in the district. Paula avoided calling the group a committee, task force, advisory team or other bureaucratic or trendy name. The group was being organized to think about teaching and learning; so, the name selected was "think group."

Paula called each selected teacher later in the same day that she sent the e-mail. There were concerns about how much time this work would take and how much good this work could really do. Paula heard some genuine expressions of frustration and caution: "I'm just so busy already" and "I have no interest in helping create an easily forgotten and quickly forgotten report." Paula assured the four teachers that the think group really would think out loud with no limits or restrictions on ideas to be expressed. She coaxed, "Just come once. If it wastes your time, never come to another meeting. If it's worth your time, stay with us until we finish." All four teachers agreed to participate. The meeting was scheduled for a Tuesday afternoon at 4:30 in Mr. Prather's classroom, and Paula brought some snacks. The conversation began on time and immediately got to the heart of the matter.

Paula Hammisch: Thank you for coming to this meeting. Our purpose is clear. We need to determine why the test scores in our school district are not showing the necessary progress. The elementary schools began a similar process last year; their work and ours may at some point be combined, but for now we will concentrate on middle school and high school. The goal is to increase test scores, which, as you know, have been disappointing in our school district in recent years. To be blunt, our schools' scores are unacceptable. So, what thoughts do you have on how we can improve the scores on the state assessment tests?

Jason Prather: I think about this a lot. Here's my first idea. It's not about the test scores. It's about learning, which means that it's about teaching. I suppose there are some short-term actions you can take to get test scores to jump up for one year. You know how a soft drink maker or other company offers a great deal, maybe buy one get one free? Their sales go way up for a few weeks, but when that promotion is over, sales might go back down to normal. There's a lot more than that to getting your product sales to increase year after year. The best way to do that is to have a better product than any of your competitors and then to continue to make it better.

For us in school the comparison would be, are we teaching the best possible way this year? And then, are we making improvements in how we teach as new ideas and new methods are shown to be more effective? If you ask me, when the subject is how to increase test scores, the answer is simple—it's the teaching. It's the teaching and it's the teaching. If we teach in ways that cause each student to learn, then the test scores will go up. But we cannot get obsessed with test scores. We can and should get obsessed with teaching and with learning. When we get the teaching and the learning right, the test scores will skyrocket to new levels.

Katie Fletcher: I understand what Jason is saying, and I have used every possible teaching method I know of, but there are so many students who just don't care about school that getting test scores up may be impossible. Getting them to do homework is like getting them to climb a mountain. Getting them to come to class prepared to learn, or at least to pay attention, is more difficult every day. Sure, some of my students in the French III class are fluent. They care, they work, they think, they try and they cooperate. They have taken full advantage of the opportunities I've given them. I give all the other students the same opportunities, but so many of them do nothing. They don't turn in homework. They don't prepare for tests. They skip class. They skip school. I call their parents or guardians, and some try to help, but others just say they cannot control their child at home either. Now, with those realities, how can we get test scores up? Jason, you've been in my classroom once to visit. You know the teaching was good. Yeah, it's the teaching and the learning, but it's also the students' work ethic and their cooperation that matter. I'm fed up with apathetic, disruptive students. If their education and their test scores mean nothing to them, what more can I do?

Angela Overstreet: I've been teaching for 22 years. I've seen these trends before. The state is making us take these tests each year, and they publish the results in the newspapers. I'm not sure what the real motive is. Is the state trying to embarrass people? We've had to take other tests over the years—and some were used for a long time, but others were abandoned. If we put a lot of time and work into some new plan to get these test scores up and in a year or two the state decides to use a different test, we will have wasted lots of time. Teachers know that these tests are like other changes in schools that we've seen over the years. Most of them last for a few years and then they're gone. Does anyone remember the new math? What a waste of time that was. Schools bought new books and teachers went to endless training so the students could be taught the new math. And nobody uses that anymore. I teach today the same way I taught 22 years ago. I do what my college professor of education taught me. He warned us to beware of fads and trends. Sure, I want the students to do well, but let's not turn the school upside down just because of some excitement over scores on tests that may not be used in a few years.

Ken Belton: Every year the test scores get announced. Some schools show improvement, some stay the same, and some get worse. I never did think that one number could tell you much about a school. If a school scores 51 this year and scored 50 last year, what does that really tell you? Did every student do a little bit better? Did a few students do a lot better and some others did awful, but the overall number went up because of a few superstar students doing really well? I see it year after year. Some students make great grades and they always did, and they probably always will. Some students do average work and, you guessed it, they always have and they probably will forever. The students who do poorly are often the students who have always done poorly. No matter what we try, year after year, they still fail or just barely pass. The test scores squeeze all of these results from all of these students into one number. How can that really mean much?

I think we should look at how each student does, not at how some test says the entire school did. We don't do that with anything else in school. We don't give students one grade based on all the work they did during the entire year. We give them grades on homework, on tests, on assignments and on their report cards. Even in sports or in other extracurricular activities, we don't take just one number and say that tells you everything you need to know. We keep score in sports and we keep lots of other statistics. The high school marching band is not evaluated on how they do on one note they play in one song during one presentation. They have a full season of performances and of competitions. So, I can see what Jason is saying, but maybe I see it that way for other reasons. It's not about the test scores. No one test score can tell you enough to really make a decision or reach a conclusion.

Paula Hammisch: What you are saying makes sense. Your perspectives are genuine and honest. I appreciate your convictions and your opinions. But we still have to deal with the reality that our state places major emphasis on how the students in each school do on one set of tests. There are some other factors that go into the total, final, comprehensive number, but the major factor is how the students do on the several days' worth of tests we take each year. Granted, those tests are imperfect. We've revised what we teach to match what we're told the tests will be about. We teach our students much more than that, of course, but we really have worked hard in this district to make sure that our students are taught what the tests are supposed to measure. We've done a lot of work to be sure that our students know more than facts, facts and extra facts.

We've emphasized thinking skills, reasoning, explaining and writing. The parts of the tests that require longer answers with students reaching conclusions and giving their reasons, well, we've worked on that for years in our school district. But still, according to the tests, we make progress in some schools some years and no progress in other schools. Each school in our district has made progress since the first year of testing, but some schools have gone up and down. Some schools have made tiny steps of progress only to lose some of that in one year and wonder what they did wrong. We're supposed to do better on the test scores each year. One year from now, the test score of each school in this district has to be higher than it is now. How do we do that?

Katie Fletcher: You want to know the truth? It probably cannot happen. I know you don't want to hear that and I know that an assistant superintendent can't go back to the superintendent and say the goal cannot be reached. So, here's a different answer. Find out what successful schools in the state are doing and copy their ideas and their actions. Jason mentioned soft drink companies. They borrow ideas and actions from each other all the time. Businesses see what their competitors are doing and they learn from them. So, let's pick two or three schools that have made improvements in their test scores and let's see what they did. Then let's copy their successful actions—of course, with a few adjustments for unique situations here. Let's not reinvent anything. Let's do what other people who have figured out the secrets to these tests have done. I know we've already borrowed some ideas from other schools, but there must be more lessons that have been learned around the state.

Jason Prather: That could help, Katie, In fact, the state's department of education sent a team of teachers out to do exactly what you suggested. Their report is on the state website, and our principal has a copy of it in the office. You know what it says?

Katie Fletcher: Let me guess. It said that the only three things that matter were the teaching and the teaching and the teaching. Did you write the report, Jason? You know I'm teasing you, but you also know that I am very serious about my teaching. I work extra hours. I stay late to help students who are willing to work extra. I've called parents and guardians. I've visited some students' homes. I've done it all, and the response from so many students is nothing, zero, zip. I am thankful for the students who do respond to me, but for the other students, well, they gave up on school years ago and I can't change that. I regret their decision to do nothing, but having tried for three years to move them, to awaken them, to encourage them, to jump start their brains. I get nowhere.

Jason Prather: It *is* frustrating. It *is* discouraging. It *is* unfair to you. It *is* disappointing, but I think there is an answer. I think we can make working at school more rewarding for you and more meaningful for students.

Ken Belton: Jason, if you think you can outsmart the bell-shaped curve, you are either a dreamer or are going to win the Nobel Prize. Students come to middle school and to high school already set in their ways. You check the grades of 6th graders and then check the grades of those same students when they are high school seniors. You know what you'll find? The same students are making the honor roll year after year. The same students are making average grades; the same students are barely getting by. Plus the ones who flunked 6th grade are not there anymore by high school. They've quit. They've dropped out. That's just the way it is.

Angela Overstreet: Well, that really is too bad, but it's true. I've had some students for two consecutive years, and they didn't do any better the second time than the first time. I did exactly what I did the first time. They should have remembered it. They should have had an advantage. Nothing was new. But they showed no improvement. I think we give all of our students the same opportunity to learn, but some of them just will not try. Plenty of my students have done just fine and the others, well, I know I tried, but I don't think they tried very hard at all.

Jason Prather: Here's my question. Are the students good at anything? I don't mean just at school, I mean are they good at anything in any part of their lives? If they are old enough, have they learned how to drive a car and did they get a driver's license? If they play a sport, are they better in the sport than they used to be? If they have a job, are they good enough at the job to not get fired, to not quit, and to keep working so they get paid? Do the students have hobbies and activities outside of school that they work at? You know, do they play games with friends; are they experts on computers; are they involved in something at their church; do they help their family with chores around the house; do they volunteer their time in the community; do they sometimes baby-sit for a younger sister or brother; do they like movies and do they know all the details about some movie star; do they like sports and can they recite endless sports statistics; do they think that space travel is neat and would they like to go into space?

My point is that every student is interested in something, is good at something and cares about something. If we connect school with wholesome topics that students are already interested in, are good at, care about, hey, they can see some reason to work at school. If they work more and harder at school they will learn more, and if they learn more, their test scores will go up. But the goal should not be to get scores up. The goal is to get students to learn more by getting them to commit to school and then, you know what? Test scores would go up as a result of making school seem real and worthwhile and meaningful right now to students.

Paula Hammisch: That's quite an idea, Jason. It might be hard to argue with, but we need some details. How do you make school work the way you described it if we connect everything with what students are interested in, already know about, are good at and already care about? What does that do to curriculum and to teaching methods and to how we train teachers and to everything else?

Ken Belton: Yeah, well, here's my question for you, Jason. If all we do is what students care about, we could have nothing but movies and games and entertainment, and then test scores would drop straight down.

Jason Prather: I see what you mean. I really understand your concerns. It took some time for me to become convinced, but I learned it from watching the students. You remember when that new skateboarding park opened? Here's how it works at that park. The rules are put up on a big board, but the children and teenagers who are there do much more than just follow those posted rules. They take turns. They help people get up after a fall. They talk to each other and give ideas on how to improve in skateboarding and on rollerblades. They acknowledge great achievements by the most accomplished skaters. They also acknowledge newcomers when they complete the simplest stunts.

Katie Fletcher: Come on Jason, what's all that got to do with getting test scores up and with getting students to make commitments to school? What's all that got to do with teaching and with learning? Are you suggesting that we need a skateboard park at each school?

Jason Prather: Neat idea, Katie. I wish that could be done, but the students probably could find a way to turn the parking lots into skateboard parks themselves if we game them the materials, the chance, the time and the guidance. That's the point. If we let them make a skateboard park here at school, some of the students who never do anything, who never do homework, who never pay attention in class and who are ready to drop out would work harder than we have ever seen them work.

Paula Hammisch: Jason, I'm still not sure where you're going with this. How would building a skateboard park make sure that our students are fully ready for the state tests each year? I can see that there could be some math connections and some science connections with the designing and the building of a skateboard park, but the state tests are more than that.

Jason Prather: Well, a few years ago I began wondering why so many students about middle school age start giving up on school and begin heading toward becoming 16-year-old high school dropouts. As soon as they were 16 and dropped out of school, many of them seemed to get the first job they could find and to really work at it. How could they go from doing nothing for years at school to getting a job and taking it seriously? So I asked them. They said the job was real. They said that school had nothing to do with their real lives. Then I started asking teachers at workshops and conferences to answer a question for me. The question was, "Think of the best teacher you ever had. What did this teacher do that made him or her the best?" Guess what people always say?

Angela Overstreet: I can imagine. They said their best teacher made school fun. But Jason, school is work. We can't have recess all day. We can't show movies all day. We can't give the students long lunch periods just to visit with friends and have fun. School is not fun. School is work.

Jason Prather: Exactly. So is skateboarding. Those students who don't work at school are the same human beings who work and work and work at becoming great skateboarders. While they work they are having fun, but they do work. They fall down and they get back up. That's no fun, but they persist. They practice and practice. They talk about it. They think about it. They learn from each other. They read about it. They commit themselves to improving. Lots of what they do with skateboarding or any other hobby is not fun; it's work, but they eagerly do it. Why? Because it's real and because it matters to them right now and that makes it worth working on with total commitment.

Ken Belton: What did all those teachers who spoke to you at workshops say about what their best teachers did?

Jason Prather: Exactly what you and I would say about our best teacher: The teacher made learning connect with real life right now. They also said that the teacher cared about them, was enthusiastic about teaching and used many different teaching methods. Still, what came through most often and most clearly was that great teachers have always made learning connect with real life right now. I've come to realize that our students are real people who are living real lives right now. But that's not how we usually teach them. We tell elementary students, you need to learn what we teach because you'll need it in middle school. We tell middle school students, you need to learn this because you'll need it in high school. We tell high school students, you need to learn this because you'll need it in college or in vocational school or at work. Learning at school is always something that we tell students they'll need at some vague later time. But students live right now, at this moment. School needs to matter right now, at this moment. Every subject we teach to every student can connect with the real lives that students are living now.

Paula Hammisch: Maybe that could work. Students play games, and there is usually some math involved with every game. You could show how many spaces you move your game piece. You count the yards to go to get a first down. You count the seconds left in the basketball game. I guess there's a lot of science in hitting a baseball. Newspapers write stores about sporting events, so that connects sports with language arts. Social studies classes could examine how games or sports were invented and what games or sports ancient civilizations played. Jason, there might be something here. And, you know, our school district really has done everything those other top ten schools in the state with the highest test scores have done. Maybe we can do some of that better, but no top ten school district is doing anything we haven't already tried or that we haven't already been trained in. There may be a much simpler idea that is also a much bigger idea. Make school real. Make school connect with the lives of students now. What does everyone think?

Angela Overstreet: Well, I know how to teach. I know what I was taught about how to teach. That overhead projector and I have presented information to students for 22 years, and we will continue to do that until I retire. Every student can see what I put on the projector. They can write it down. They can memorize it. They can put it in answers on tests. Now if you want me to show students more about how what we do in class is part of everyday life, that would be pretty easy to do. I could make some new overhead transparency sheets, but I still need to keep using what I've always used. That's what I was taught.

Ken Belton: I'm not so sure the results will vary much, but I'd rather try what Jason is saying than start all over with some new, strange idea that some expert will come here to teach us. Whenever we fall for the latest fad, we end up wasting lots of time and money, and then in a few years we have to try something else and another new expert comes in, and everyone just gets tired of all that. Maybe something as simple as showing students how learning connects with what they already know and with what they already do could help. I had a few great teachers and, you know, come to think of it, that's pretty much what they did. They made learning interesting and fascinating because it applied to real life.

Katie Fletcher: I hope it works for all of you. My plans are set. As soon as I can find another job, I have to leave teaching. I already try to make it real for my students. I take them to France on the Internet often. We visited the French restaurant downtown. We bring in French visitors to our town or French residents of this city to speak to the class. I make it as real as I can. What more can I do?

Jason Prather: Katie, here's what my French teacher did when I was in 9th grade. She knew that I was interested in soccer. She taught us a French vocabulary lesson all about soccer. I could discuss soccer in French! She then brought a visitor to our class: a player on the women's soccer team at the university. She talked to us in French about soccer. I was hooked! From that point on, learning French made sense because I went to some of the university soccer games and there were other French-speaking players. The whole team had learned enough French to communicate to each other on the soccer field in French. The other teams they played never quite figured it all out, so speaking French gave the soccer team an advantage. That was pretty real to me.

Katie Fletcher: It makes sense and all, but some of the students will still hate French and will still not work. I'm willing to try. Until I leave this job, I want to do it well. So, what do I do? Just ask them what they are interested in and create French lessons about that?

Paula Hammisch: That's a really important question, Katie. What you're telling us, Jason, does make sense, but we need more details. Our super-intendent and school board are expecting us to create a plan and a report and some way to measure progress. What do you suggest we do to create all that?

Jason Prather: I've been teaching that way for the past two years, and the results are good. All the research I conducted with the people who told me about their best teachers inspired me to create lessons and activities for my students that begin with what students already know, with what they are already good at, with what they are already interested in and then to make connections with their knowledge, their skills, their interests and with what they need to learn in my class. It works.

I had a really memorable discussion with a few students two years ago during one of my frequent visits to the skateboard park. I asked them about ways to make connections with skateboarding, rollerblading and school. They wondered at first if it could be done. Then I asked about math. Well, they talked about the cost of a skateboard. I asked about science. They mentioned the speeds they work up to on rollerblades. From that point on it made sense to the students. They kept saying things like, "Hey, it would really be extreme if we could do that at school."

So, my students and I call it Extreme Teaching when we start with their knowledge, their talents and their interests and then make connections with what they need to know. We then take it to another extreme and find ways to apply what they learn to their life right now, and then they can see reasons to apply their learning to their life in the near future. As long as it fascinates the students now and seems real to them now, they are perfectly willing to work, to think, to explore, to analyze ideas, to read books—you name it. To use what they already know seems to bring them into the educational process as full partners who are endless resources of material because they are endless resources of experiences, ideas, and more. It works! My students have consistently shown improvement in their grades, in their attendance at school and even in how seriously they take the state tests. Can you believe that? Those state tests get a better commitment from the students because they have already made a better commitment to school.

Paula Hammisch: OK, Jason, but what do we report to the board of education and to the superintendent?

Jason Prather: Maybe I can help. I've been putting ideas about Extreme Teaching on paper. I'd be glad to share that with this group. Paula, you could show it to the superintendent. Katie, Angela and Ken could show it to their colleagues at their schools. We could meet again in a month or so and everyone could tell us what the reactions were to the idea and the methods of Extreme Teaching. Would that make sense?

Paula Hammisch: Ken, Angela, Katie, is that OK? Heads are nodding yes, so that's our plan. Jason will get each of us a copy of his Extreme Teaching materials. We'll show it to our colleagues. Maybe each of you can use it in your classrooms. We will meet one month from today and update each other. Thanks for you time and your help today.

CHAPTER 2

Opportunity and Challenge

Jason Prather eagerly accepted his assignment. Jason thinks about teaching whenever he is not in a classroom. When Jason goes to a grocery store, to a sporting event, to a golf course, to a movie, to church or to most any other place, he often looks for ideas that could be used in his classroom. Just as some department stores offer special prices at certain times (such as for people who shop early on a Saturday morning), Jason offers special homework deals—turn in your homework one day early and get bonus points. Movie theaters show previews of coming attractions; Jason creates video previews of what his classes will do the next week and he shows these two-minute previews at the end of class on Friday. The students love the previews and really benefit from the advance information. Jason often includes students in the production of videos, and one student went from doing a video project for Jason to actually being paid for being in a local television commercial. Making connections with real life for teaching ideas and for the benefit of students is a high priority for Jason Prather.

Jason realized early in his teaching career that the middle school students he knows and the high school students he teaches are real people who are living real lives right now. Jason also realized rather early in his teaching career that for many, if not most, middle school and high school students, the academic experiences at school are barely tolerable, are often hated, are usually boring and rarely seem to relate in any meaningful, clear and immediate way to the current, real and dynamic lives that students live right now.

So, Jason began adjusting how he taught, not what he taught. Jason knew he could not stray from the required curriculum of the school, school district and state; he was responsible for teaching the approved curriculum in its entirety in his subject area. He also knew that he was expected to strengthen his students' skills in areas that go across all subject content topics, skills such as reading, writing, thinking and use of math.

Teachers usually have a range of teaching methods to use, and Jason's range expanded annually. His range of teaching methods grew most dramatically after he watched a soccer game that included several of his high school students and after he went to a high school marching band competition. Jason reached conclusions then that forever changed how he teaches, why he teaches and what he is satisfied with as successful teaching.

For Jason Prather, the idea of learning is much bigger than the typical idea of, structure of, content of, organization of and experience of school. For Jason, this revelation meant that his idea of teaching, his method of teaching, his effectiveness as a teacher had to expand to reach the depth, width, breadth, power, creativity and dynamic of the totality of learning. Put simply, the typical middle school and high school experience, which relies on textbooks, worksheets and videos, produces at best a limited portion of what complete learning is. Schools can do more; schools can do better. Jason accepted the challenging opportunity to make his classroom a place where teaching caused learning, where teaching methods created learning experiences that took students to the extremes of knowledge, reasoning, memory, reflection, information, skills, thought, achievement and wisdom. To cause such extreme learning by all of his students, Jason Prather realized that he must daily do the most effective Extreme Teaching possible. It is this dedication to Extreme Teaching, which causes extreme learning by students, that energizes, renews and inspires Jason Prather. Teaching has never been the same for Jason Prather since he began using the methods and the perspective of Extreme Teaching. The impact of Extreme Teaching on Jason Prather's students is actually greater than the impact on Jason, because the students' natural, emerging and inherent energy, curiosity, creativity and ability are now matched with fascinating and meaningful experiences.

What extreme insight did Jason Prather gain by attending a high school soccer game and a high school marching band contest? How did Jason gain this extreme insight? He watched, he asked, he listened, he reflected, he concluded, and he took action. Following are his thoughts about this process.

JASON PRATHER'S CONVICTIONS AND CONCLUSIONS

I hear what teachers say in moments of disappointment and frustration. I hear them question their career choice. I hear their confusion about personal goals and career goals when they are 50 percent of the way to retirement but 100 percent of the way to giving up on teaching. I hear the expressions of joy, success and celebration from some teachers, but the number of those teachers seems to be decreasing.

I hear what students say in moments of disappointment and frustration, in times of anger and rebellion. I hear their confusion about personal goals and school goals when they are 75 percent or more of the way to high school graduation but 100 percent of the way to giving up on school. I hear the expressions of joy, success and celebration from some students, usually because of athletics or other extracurricular activities or because of being with friends. Still, the number of students who seek high academic achievement and who are thrilled with high academic achievement seems to be decreasing.

What went wrong? I have watched middle school students and high school students at lunch in the school cafeteria. I have watched them at sporting events and at marching band contests. I have listened to them in the hallways. In all of these settings, what I see and what I hear— wow, it is vibrant. I've seen teachers interact with the students in these same settings, and it is vibrant. So if everyone is excited about and dedicated to great achievements in sports, in marching band contests, in school theater productions and in every other energetic extracurricular activity, why are those same people not as excited and dedicated to learning in classrooms at school?

I have a perspective on this. The routines and procedures, the processes and the activities associated with the academic side of school are far too often ordinary, meaningless, boring and of little use. Far too often, school means for teachers and students a lowest common denominator, a paint-by-numbers, generic, plain vanilla, 50th-percentile, average, bureaucratic ordeal that is to be endured. There is school and there is real, meaningful, interesting, fascinating, purposeful life, but real life and the academic part of school seem to have little in common. That is unfortunate.

Middle school students are geared to live in extremes. For a middle school student, today's best friend can become tomorrow's worst enemy. There is not much neutrality in the life of a middle school-aged person. Likes are usually strong likes. Dislikes are usually strong dislikes. However, a like can become a dislike with little or no warning. "But math was always your favorite subject," a confused adult says to a 7th grader. "Yeah, but I hate math now. The teacher doesn't like me. She picks on me. I hate math."

High school students are also geared to live in extremes. "I need a job. I've got to get a job." So, the 16-year-old gets a job and quits in two weeks. "It was no fun. I was bored." The translation of those thoughts could mean "My girlfriend said I had to spend more time with her or we'd break up, so I quit my job for her and in a month we broke up anyway."

Middle school students and high school students seek the extremes of life, are geared toward the extremes of life. Sure, adults have to show some 11- to 19-year-olds that some extremes can be unsafe, risky, illegal, immoral, destructive and unwise; however, adults should not subdue all the extreme inclinations of young people. In fact, some of those extreme tendencies can be applied and guided in ways that are beneficial, wholesome, useful, creative, successful and productive.

When I was a student teacher, I once asked 8th graders to give the three-word completion of this statement: "A rose by any other name would _____ _____ _____." Their creative replies were as good or better than Shakespeare's original wording: "not be one," "cause massive riots," "change everything forever," "be something else," and "still be red."

Those same students participated in an interdisciplinary project to create a fictional presidential candidate named Mario Bradleynunn. The name came from three people who chose not to run for president in 1988: New York governor Mario Cuomo, New Jersey senator Bill Bradley and Georgia senator Sam Nunn. From speeches to posters, from a campaign theme song to campaign commercials, the students created the entire campaign. The presidential debates in the classroom were more memorable, more profound and more to the point than what passes as the standard version of adult political debates. The campaign activities went to extremes, but that experience was more meaningful and more certain to cause learning than "Read the chapter about presidential elections. Answer all questions at the end of the chapter. Complete this practice quiz. Watch this video. Take this test."

From my years of working directly with students, of listening closely to students and of intensely observing students, some conclusions and some convictions have emerged. From the perspective of many middle school students and high school students—those 11- to 19-year-olds whose lives are inherently and naturally, wonderfully and boldly, energetically and creatively, sometimes wisely and sometimes unwisely inclined toward adventurous extremes—school is far too often a predictable and pedantic pattern of being told to sit down, be quiet, read textbooks, answer questions at the end of each chapter, complete some generic worksheets, take some superficial tests each Friday and, if you endure this routine for enough years, you will earn the title of high school graduate.

When not in classrooms at school but still at school—perhaps in the cafeteria or at a club meeting, perhaps in the hallways between classes or at a sports practice, perhaps while waiting for a bus ride home or at a school group's fundraising car wash—many students who appear to be lethargic in classes emerge as endlessly energetic people who vibrantly interact, who willingly work and who eagerly make a commitment. What is it about the classroom part of school that far too often dulls the inherent vitality of students and frustrates the hopeful efforts of teachers? What is it about the other parts of school that applies and inspires the inherent vitality of students? Can this provide any ideas for reaching the academic priorities of teachers who wish those same students would work as hard and show as much life in the classroom?

One common question, complaint and criticism from students in regard to some classes they take at school is "When are we ever going to need this?" That question could be about a list of prepositions to memorize, an algebra equation to help solve a dreaded "word problem," a scientific formula about force and mass, an 18th-century political debate about the proposed constitution for the 13 states, or a lesson about different painting styles of French artists. "I'm going to repair cars in my uncle's auto shop after I finish school. French artists have nothing to do with that, so I just don't care. This is boring. I'm not doing this."

Consider football as an example of the different perspectives that some students have about the classroom part of school and the extracurricular part of school. In football, athletes learn to block and tackle. Those same students who might ask about the usefulness of a scientific formula about force and mass will not question the coach who gives the signal to begin the next block and tackle drill. But "When will you need that?" could be asked of these students. "As you live your life day to day, year to year, decade to decade, when will you ever apply the skills of blocking and tackling?" Except for the tiny percentage of high school football players who do play in college, the answer to the question is "never after high school." "Well," one might ask the student, "if all the work you are doing to master blocking and tackling serves no purpose and has no use after high school, why are you working so hard at it?"

At that moment the high school student might pause, reflect, look us in the eye, and very politely say, "Well, because it's real to me. It matters to me. Plus, I do use it every Friday night at games that big crowds come to watch. They cheer our blocks and tackles. We win games. We win trophies. We feel important. So, it's all pretty cool."

Notice, the student we "spoke" with here never mentioned the application of a scientific formula about force and mass to the skills of blocking and tackling. Rather, the student reminded us that football is real because it is played in public, because large crowds watch the games, because rewards are given and because it is celebrated. If it is real, if it matters now, if it is rewarded in the ways that our society rewards what we appear to really value (such as large, cheering crowds; significant media coverage; awards and financial gain measured in college scholarships; and press conferences attended by high school coaches, high school athletes, the college coach and many news reporters), then students realize that the activity must be real. In this case, students follow the aphorism "We get more of what we reward."

In schools, the biggest rewards, the biggest celebrations, the biggest crowds, the biggest trophies, the biggest news stories are for athletic teams and marching bands. Students give schools more of what schools reward most—touchdowns, three-point shots, home runs and halftime music extravaganzas. Athletic achievements and marching band achievements are treated as beneficial, worthwhile, wholesome and exciting. The point here is not to belittle those good results; the point is to realize how much extreme commitment, interest, work and support those activities inspire from students and to duplicate or surpass that commitment for classroom learning. It can be done, and any willing teacher can do it.

Football is real to many students, including those who participate and who watch. Football must be real to parents and guardians, who often attend games in much larger numbers than they attend math competitions to watch, cheer and reward math scholars. Does that sound absurd? Only because it sounds so unusual, but what a football booster group of parents and guardians can do to support athletes could be matched by a math booster group. What would the results be? Let's find out!

Students are real people who are living real lives right now. Students are extreme people living extreme lives right now. From liking the most extreme new fashion to liking the most extreme new music, from wanting to see the most extreme new movie to mastering the most extremely complex new computer software, from the extremes of joy to despair in little time, from the extremes of total commitment to total disinterest, from the extremes of cooperation to rebellion, if it is real and if it is really extreme, middle school and high school students can and will totally commit themselves to it. Classroom experiences can be real, can be really extreme, can be totally committed to, can be inspiring for students, can cause learning by students, can be created by teachers and can be rewarding for teachers. When extreme teaching causes extreme learning, everyone benefits.

I know there will be a complaint from some teachers about using rewards. "You mean we have to give the students rewards to get them to study? They should learn because it is important."

OK, let's use that approach with football: No spectators may come to games. No scoreboard will be used. No score will be kept. No letters and jackets will be earned. No statistics will be kept. No postseason banquets will be held. No pep rallies will be allowed. No homecoming parade or celebration will take place. No trophies will be earned. Does that make sense? It does if people should play football just because they should see the importance of wanting to block and tackle well for the inherent reward of blocking and tackling well. But people expect to attend sporting events to cheer, to see the scoreboard and to watch the marching band perform at halftime, to attend pep rallies and to celebrate the football homecoming event. In the classroom learning part of the school experience, the thinking is different, for reasons that appear to me to be unacceptable. If the purpose of school really is to cause learning—which primarily means academic learning of the vital intellectual skills and subjects—then the biggest, most obvious, most public and most celebrated rewards should be based on academic achievement. We should keep every wholesome award, reward, tradition and ceremony associated with extracurricular events but surpass those awards with a new and improved recognition of student academic achievement.

Let's back up and look very directly into the lives of 11- to19-year-olds in the United States. When not at school, many people in the 11–19 age group are eagerly, enthusiastically and successfully learning, achieving, trying, exploring, making sense of, discovering, interacting, thinking, communicating and progressing in beneficial ways in worthwhile endeavors.

What is it about school that makes it so, well, schoolish? By *schoolish*, I mean why is school usually so ordinary, routine, predictable, plain, traditional, unreal, uninspiring and disconnected? Why are so many classes and classroom activities so superficial, simplistic and forgettable?

Students have their very certain, precise and piercing answer to that question: "School is boring." That is the concise way for teenagers to express the sentiment "School is the same thing every year. You know, teachers talk at us, give us textbooks to read, make copies of worksheets for us to fill out, give us tests and pretty much keep us under control with busywork."

Teachers have their very certain and very genuine answer to this: "So many more students just will not work or think or try. Even if we do something different in class, many students just don't care or, just as bad, they get wild and I have to put them all right back into the text-book and worksheet procedures to manage and control them."

Imagine the 20th reunion of a high school class. Smiles, hugs and handshakes are exchanged. Stories and laughs and tears are shared. Spouses are introduced and pictures of children are shown. Some teachers from 20 years ago attend. One teacher, Ms. Seward, is approached by a smiling 38-year-old lady who says, "Ms. Seward. Hello, Ms. Seward. I'm Kim McIntyre. I was Kim Bell in high school. You were my favorite teacher." Ms. Seward smiles politely and sincerely, "Kim, dear Kim, it's so good to see you. You look wonderful. I hope that life has been good to you."

Kim looks Ms. Seward deeply in the eyes and says, "Ms. Seward, I want you to know that the worksheet you handed out in September of my senior year really changed my life."

Of course that will never happen. Worksheets do not change lives. Simplistic, generic, mass-produced, copy machine-duplicated, name-less, faceless, purposeless, often worthless worksheets never really change the life of any student for the better. Yes, conscientious teachers can *create* thinksheets, which help cause learning; however, far too many worksheets used in far too many classes are of limited, perhaps little, or no real value. What does change the lives of students for the better? In my judgment and experience, students' lives are changed by extreme teachers who do extreme teaching that causes extreme learning.

Ask a group of ten adults to respond to this question: "What is the purpose of a school?" The question is not about the school's goal for this year or the action plans for this year. The question is not about the lofty words of a school's mission statement but about the purpose of a school: the essential reason that a school exists. The ten replies would probably be similar to these:

1. To prepare children for the duties of citizenship and family responsibility.
2. To teach the basics of reading, writing and math.
3. To prepare students for the jobs that they will have in the future.
4. To educate the whole child.
5. To meet the academic, social and overall growing-up needs of students.

6. To prepare a new generation to be leaders of our community and workers in our community.
7. To instill values of democracy, free enterprise and love of knowledge.
8. To show students how to live as law-abiding citizens.
9. To teach students how to learn so they can learn for a lifetime.
10. To help each student reach his or her potential.

What is common across those ten statements? There are some references to education, knowledge and learning. There are other references to citizenship, democracy, jobs and community responsibilities. To be blunt, concise, clear and to the point, the ten statements could be concisely merged into the aphorism "The purpose of a school is to cause learning."

Let's repeat this basic, fundamental truth: The purpose of a school is to cause learning. Causing learning—intended, curriculum-based, worthwhile, meaningful, real, useful, fascinating learning caused by intended, designed, interactive, energetic, creative, real, fascinating classroom lessons and activities—is the measurement standard against which school decisions, resources, efforts and results should be evaluated. Make the decision that will best cause learning. Apply resources in the ways that best cause learning. Direct your efforts toward the work that will best cause learning. Insist on results that confirm that learning was caused, that learning did happen.

Are schools causing learning? Are all schools causing all students to learn? Are students learning all they are able to learn? Are some students learning some academic material, ideas, information and skills at school while other students learn more and still others learn less? What keeps more students in more schools from learning all that they should and could learn? Of all the variables that impact student learning and that educators can control, the variable that matters most is the effectiveness of teaching.

What is teaching? Teaching is that collection of designed activities that, when fully and properly implemented, will cause the desired learning to occur. To condense that idea, we can say that teaching causes learning. If students do not learn, teaching did not happen. If all students do not learn all they should learn, then all of the teaching that needed to occur did not happen. There may have been some activity, talking, work, tests and grades in the classroom, but only if the intended learning happened in sufficient quantity and quality can we say that teaching happened. Without sufficient quantity and quality of learning occurring in a classroom, what took place there was merely schooling.

What is schooling? It is what students most dislike about school. It is what conscientious teachers most dislike about school. Schooling is going through the motions of schoolish activities with little real thinking, real interaction, real creativity, real reasoning, real brain-expanding reflection, real acquisition of useful information that is worth remembering or real learning.

Students of my generation asked our middle school and high school teachers the inevitable questions: "When am I going to use this? How will Shakespeare help me get a job? What difference does it make if I know the parts of a cell? What good does it do me now to know about some discovery hundreds of years ago?"

Those questions were answered with responses based on a timed-release justification of education: "Well, you need to know this so you will be ready for your classes next year," or "You will need this in college," or "You never know what job you might have someday, so we need to prepare you for everything."

Students in my generation disliked those answers, but we accepted the reality that no better answers would be offered. Some of us who chose teaching as a career or who were chosen by teaching promised to give our students experiences at school that would be so obviously meaningful, useful, real and fascinating that questions of relevance would be minimized or prevented. Timed-release education is just not good enough. Learn it today, or at least pass a test on it today, because at some vague moment in the uncertain future that cannot be predicted accurately, you will need to know this. If that timed-release justification of education was ever acceptable, it is no longer adequate and probably never was truly convincing or sufficient.

The children of people I was in school with are in a generation that asks their middle school and high school teachers a much more demanding, important, practical and real question about what schools expect students to learn. The updated question is "What am I going to do in my life right now with what the school says I have to learn?"

Notice the difference in urgency, in the realism, in the conviction and in the challenge issued by the two questions. One generation acquiesced to the timed-release justification for and rationalization of school, education, homework, tests and textbooks. "You'll need this later in school or later in life" was accepted. It should be noted that the timed-release standard implies that school is not really life but is preparation for real living in an undated future.

A new generation requests, expects and deserves that school be useful, meaningful, worthwhile and worth committing to now, for benefits now, for application now and for connections with the real life that a student is living now. This standard acknowledges that, as I've said before, students are real people who are living real lives right now.

Educators can thank students for expecting what they learn at school and how they learn it to be real right now; to matter right now; to be worthwhile right now; to be worth committing to right now; to be fascinating right now; and to be worth the time, effort and brain power of students right now.

The first complaint of educators, parents, guardians and other adults to this idea will likely be "You mean that school should just be fun for students all the time?" No. Double no. Fun while learning at school is a lovely by-product of fascination. When teachers fascinate students who then commit themselves to working and to learning, the school adventure seems to be fun. We do not expect middle school or high school students to say, "Hey, that science class provided higher-order thinking experiences that enabled me to probe, analyze and organize information into compelling and practical conclusions." A more likely teenage version of that statement would be, "Well, you know, it was pretty interesting. We did neat experiments. I got an A and we had some fun."

The second complaint of adults is probably "So, we can only teach what is new and up to date?" Wrong. We teach Plato's ideas, Columbus's exploration, Newton's laws of science, Euclid's concepts of geometry, Shakespeare's words and ideas, the Declaration of Independence, the Roman civilization, international languages, the presidency of Lincoln and other treasured topics of the recent past or distant past. The difference is that in Extreme Teaching we connect those bodies of knowledge, ideas, concepts, experiences, trials and errors with the real lives that students are living today. We do not say "Well, I had to memorize the Preamble to the Constitution, plus some very smart people wrote it back in the 1780s, so you have to memorize it too. Get busy and know it by Friday."

Rather, an Extreme Teacher could say, "When 'we, the people of the United States' began the new national government, there were thirteen states and three million people and the nation was united against a common enemy, but there were already some differences emerging among the states. What has changed since then? How about population—how many people live here now and who are those people?" From that discussion starter there are endless connections that could be made to life today. Does the school have a constitution or similar governing document? Can students impact the content of that document and the application of its provisions?

An increasing number of middle school and high school students make little commitment to school. An increasing number of teachers are frustrated because so many middle school and high school students just will not take schoolwork seriously, do the work, pay attention or cooperate. An increasing number of students see school as boring, unreal, not worth the effort. An increasing number of teachers wonder how to get students to do the work.

Make school real. Make school matter. Connect what the school curriculum needs students to learn with the wholesome, beneficial and fundamental aspects of what students already know, already are interested in, already care about, already are good at and already are committed to. Make new learning at school an extension of the real life that the student has lived thus far, so that school applies meaningfully to the life the student is living now. Note that this can also show a student that years of school can connect with life during school and with life after the end of the school year, thus satisfying the advocates of timed-release education.

JASON PRATHER'S CONVICTIONS AND CONCLUSIONS: REFLECTIONS BY PAULA HAMMISCH

How does school become real in the classroom? Jason is convinced that Extreme Teaching is one way. Jason and you, the reader, will explore the personality of and the profile of Extreme Teaching in the next chapter. For now, two other complaints must be addressed: more work for teachers, and unhealthy interests of students.

Extreme Teaching is a different way of creating classroom activities, but it is not an additional task. The current results in education are perhaps improving versus recent years, but more progress is needed. Do teachers prefer bureaucratic requirements or creative, meaningful, fascinating, interactive adventures in the classroom? As Extreme Teaching helps get results for teacher and students, the need for another bureaucratic reform of education could be prevented or minimized. Extreme Teaching is one way for teachers to help lead a school to real reform of education so that learning is caused.

Jason knows that some students bring some unhealthy, illegal or immoral interests with them to school. Extreme Teaching does not embrace every interest or skill of every student. Extreme Teachers do edit, do select, do control and do generally do the responsible work of an adult who is in charge.

At a training conference he once attended, Jason Prather heard a teacher describe being asked by a school administrator to explain what the ultimate reform of education would be. The administrator expected that teacher to refer to more money, new buildings, frequent tests, bonus pay, different schedules for the school year, new laws, some additional staffing at schools or smaller class sizes so teachers could work with fewer students. Instead, the teacher replied with two words: effective teaching. Jason thought about that at length and was inspired to provide details, so he wrote the following words.

EFFECTIVE TEACHING AS THE ULTIMATE EDUCATIONAL REFORM

Why is the history of public education in the United States a history of repeated reforms? First, to our credit, we Americans are persistent people. Second, to our discredit, we continue to believe that there is an elusive law, regulation, policy, structure, process, procedure and/or bureaucracy that will finally correct any remaining imperfections in education. Persistence is honorable unless it is the persistent pursuit of that which is unproductive. Reform of laws, regulations, policies, structures, processes, procedures and/or bureaucracies is honorable unless the reform is unproved or if the reform expects law, regulations, policies, structures, processes, procedures and/or bureaucracies to do more than they can do.

So, what is a persistent, public endeavor such as education to do in the search for results? Simply stated, do effectively what matters most. In education, what matters most is the effectiveness of teaching. What is teaching? Teaching is causing learning. When schools cause learning via teaching, everyone wins and education has been successfully reformed to do what education is supposed to do.

What is a school administrator to do to guarantee that learning is caused at his or her school? Teach. Teach the teachers how to teach better. Teach the staff how to lead, how to manage and how to work better. Teach the parents and guardians how to team up with the school better. Teach the students what will be rewarded and what will be penalized. Teach a class. Teach the district's central office, the school board, the state government and the federal government about what is needed and what gets in the way. Teach—all day, every day, everyone and everywhere. Effective teaching is the ultimate reform of education. New laws are not necessarily needed. New taxes are not necessarily needed. New structural reforms are not necessarily needed. Just teach everyone, which means just cause learning to occur for and by everyone. If every educator really teaches and if every student really learns, we will have accomplished what every reform of education has sought.

We know what works in education. We know how to teach so that learning is caused. There are no valid excuses. We are interested in results only. Teach. Teach more. Teach better. Teach effectively. Teaching—that is, causing learning—is everything that school is about. So, be persistent in teaching. Be magnificently obsessed with effective teaching. Be cautious about any reform that is not devoted to effective teaching. When teaching at a school has caused every student to learn, the school is reformed and has become what it was always intended to be.

In short, effective teaching—teaching that is energetic, enthusiastic, basic, information-acquiring, skill-mastering, challenging, thought-provoking, interactive, brain-exercising, mind-expanding, personal, caring, fascinating and learning-causing—is the heart and the soul of education and, thus, is the heart and the soul of realistic education reform.

INTRODUCTION TO IMPLEMENTATION

Jason Prather's thoughts thus far are his philosophical and practical conclusions based on years of experience as a teacher. He accepted the duty to provide a plan for the committee for personal and professional reasons: Personally, he knows that what he and his students do in the classroom works; professionally, he would like to share an effective teaching method with other teachers and their students. Jason is convinced that, in education, "we know what works." No new studies are needed. No new task forces are needed. No new laws are needed. He believes that any problem facing any school has been solved in part or completely by people at another school or in another classroom. The student who refuses to work in science class during first period in room 246 eagerly works in computer class during second period in room 137. "To every problem there is an equal and opposite solution," according to Jason. When educators share success stories, the positive results can expand. That may be a simple idea, but it can create extreme results of great benefit to students and teachers. With those ideas and ideals in mind, let's turn now to Jason's explanation of how to implement Extreme Teaching.

You may have noticed that Jason Prather's conclusions and convictions are not about test scores; more specifically, his conclusions and convictions are not about increasing test scores. Why? Because Jason is convinced that if classroom experiences fascinate students, intrigue students, inspire students, build commitment from students and cause learning by students, then higher test scores will also happen. In other words, aiming at learning enables schools to hit learning and to improve test scores, but aiming at test scores alone can lead to a complete miss.

CHAPTER 3

How to Implement Extreme Teaching

Jason knew that the challenge was not to create a good idea such as Extreme Teaching. Good ideas are common. The challenge was to properly implement the good idea so good results were obtained. Jason knew that the history of public education in the United States was a history of continuous reform. The quality of the ideas of each reform varied from the spectacular to the disastrous. Still, a great idea must be implemented well or very little improvement is likely to be gained. A great idea poorly implemented gets discarded onto history's pile of what might have been.

Jason had been using the concept of Extreme Teaching, and the results were favorable. But showing other teachers how to use Extreme Teaching meant rethinking the process and procedures. The essence of Extreme Teaching is (1) connecting what students already know, already are interested in and/or already are good at (2) with what students need to know (3) using meaningful classroom activities that show and apply those connections in fascinating and real ways. Could it be that simple, Jason wondered? Is a three-step process sufficient? Jason kept reaching the same conclusion: there are indeed only three steps. Design classroom activities with the three steps and you can have a lesson planning system for Extreme Teaching.

Step 1: Identify what students know, are interested in and/or are good at that relates to the current topic in class.
Step 2: Identify what students need to know about the current topic in class.

Step 3: Create activities that will cause the desired learning by making connections with the content of step 1 and the content of step 2.

Jason began to envision a lesson plan format that uses three columns. Step 1 goes in column A. Step 2 goes in column B. Step 3 goes in column C. Could this organizational system for Extreme Teaching lesson plans really be as concise and as simple as 1, 2, 3 and A, B, C? Jason wondered. He knew that victory would be in the details of what went into the lesson plan and then in what went into the actual classroom implementation, but he hoped that a clear, user-friendly format could eas-

Table 3.1   Extreme Teaching: Lesson Plan Design for Fractions, Part 1

With this lesson, students will make connections between what they know, what they are interested in, what they are good at and *adding fractions*.

Column A	Column B	Column C
Step 1. What students know, are interested in and/or are good at that relates to this topic: • Sporting events that are divided into portions, such as the first quarter of a game or the second half of a game. • Money: 25 cents is ¼ of a dollar. Other coins can be added together. • Pizza: when cut into slices, it creates fractions of the pizza. • Age: A student who is 13½ is no longer 13 and is not yet 14. • Grades: If an A grade is 93 and your average is 92⅓, is that an A?	Step 2. What students need to learn and know: • How to add simple fractions that have a common denominator.	Step 3. Activities that will cause this learning via connections between column A and column B, along with prior learning in this class and prior/current learning in other classes. * • Use one minute of a TV sports report to show football scores by quarter. Add quarters and scores by quarter to see which quarter most impacted the outcome of the game. • Use coins—real ones or paper representations—to add quarters, dimes, nickels and pennies to create ¼ + ¼ + ¼ + ¼; ⅒ + ⅒, etc.; 1/20 + 1/20, etc.; 1/100 + 1/100, etc. • Give each student a paper pizza that has been cut into 8 equal slices; each slice is ⅛ of the pizza. Add 2 slices, 3 slices, 4 slices. Through adding all 8 slices, note the new fraction created by each addition. • Average three grades of 96½, 91, and 85½.

ily and clearly show the idea of Extreme Teaching while also showing that Extreme Teaching lesson plans were not complicated or time-consuming to create. Jason decided to put his plan to a severe test: could the Extreme Teaching system work with a topic that causes fear and frustration for many students, such as fractions? Come to think of it, he realized, teaching fractions can also cause some frustration for teachers. Maybe those mutual concerns could both be addressed with an Extreme Teaching approach to fractions. Maybe students and teachers could mutually benefit from an Extreme Teaching adventure in fractions. With that hope, Jason created a plan, which is shown in table 3.1.

The light bulb in Jason Prather's creative mind was glowing powerfully. "Wait a minute. This can be continuous. We can go beyond the extreme. One lesson using Extreme Teaching can lead directly to the next lesson. The students can learn how to add fractions and can then add that new knowledge to what they were already good at and interested in to learn how to subtract fractions."

So, Jason designed the next learning sequence using a similar format, now being able to build upon the students' newly mastered skill of adding fractions. This new skill of adding fractions goes to the top of column A in table 3.2.

Jason knew that his system of Extreme Teaching could work, but he was concerned that a teacher might look at the lesson plans above and have this response: "Well, sure, it works with math. Students have to count money. Students know the scores of sporting events. They use math all the time whether they realize it or not. And any math lessons

Table 3.2   Extreme Teaching: Lesson Plan Design for Fractions, Part 2

With this lesson, students will make connections between what they know, what they are interested in, what they are good at and *subtracting fractions*.

Column A	Column B	Column C
Step 1. What students know, are interested in and/or are good at that relates to this topic: • How to add simple fractions that have a common denominator.	Step 2. What students need to learn and know: • How to subtract simple fractions that have a common denominator.	Step 3. Activities that will cause this learning via connections between column A and column B, along with prior learning in this class and prior/current learning in other classes. * _____

continued

Table 3.2 *(continued)*

Column A	Column B	Column C
• Money: When you buy something and get change back, it can involve fractions. • Pizza: Dividing slices of a pizza between friends or family members while keeping 2 slices for later • Times recorded by athletes in a track meet or swim meet, such as 47.71 seconds versus 48.63 seconds.		• Make 100 paper coins, which will be used as pennies. Take 75 of them as the numerator and put them over a sign that reads "100" and is the denominator. The other 25 coins are over a second similar denominator. Now, subtract $^{75}/_{100} - {}^{25}/_{100} = {}^{50}/_{100}$ (this is actually done by the student removing 25 of the 75 paper coins). Use other numerators for other subtraction problems with the 100 denominator • A pizza sliced into 8 pieces = $^{8}/_{8}$, but a student takes two slices. Now there are $^{6}/_{8}$ left. Vary the number of slices taken to create other calculations. Cut another pizza into 10 pieces to work with a different denominator. • Have students walk or run around the gym floor. Record their times. Contrast the fraction part of each time, for example, 24.63 seconds and 27.42 seconds leads to subtracting $^{42}/_{100}$ from $^{63}/_{100}$.

Reminder: An Extreme Teaching lesson does not stand alone as a finite learning experience; rather, each lesson leads to other lessons or connects with other lessons. The format above is designed so one lesson connects with at least one other lesson. The lesson about adding fractions flowed easily into and connected easily with this lesson about subtracting fractions; however, the lessons could be used separately just as well as they could be used as a sequential pair.

that include anything related to pizza will get their interest. Now, what about science or language arts or social studies? What about all the other classes? How can Extreme Teaching work there?"

Jason's task became clear: Create a vast variety of Extreme Teaching lesson plans that connect with many academic subjects and school skills. Jason was convinced that students' lives included a sufficient variety of interests, talents, curiosities, skills, knowledge, competencies and expertise so that connections could be made between students' life experiences and all subjects taught at school. Jason's confidence still had to be tested, though, with the creation of lesson plans and learning sequences that show Extreme Teaching working with the wide variety of subjects taught in middle schools and high schools. The only way to accomplish this was to put the variety of lesson plans on paper. Jason said to himself, "Go for it, teacher. Get extreme." That is exactly what he did, as shown in tables 3.3–3.24 on the following pages. Each lesson plan can be used separately, but pairs of logically connected lesson plans are shown here to illustrate how an extreme learning unit or sequence can flow from the initial lesson plan.

Table 3.3 Extreme Teaching: Lesson Plan Design for Paragraph Writing, Part 1

With this lesson, students will make connections between what they know, what they are interested in, what they are good at and *writing a paragraph.*

Column A	Column B	Column C
Step 1. What students know, are interested in and/or are good at that relates to this topic: • How to communicate verbally in paragraph-length thoughts. • How to listen to paragraph-length lyrics in songs, parts of dialogue in movies, information in television commercials. • How to read paragraph-length material in newspapers, magazines, e-mail, websites, notes passed between students, handouts from teachers, printed advertisements. • How to go to restaurants or stores and read paragraph-length information on a menu, on a shelf, on a package, on a sign.	Step 2. What students need to learn and know: • How to write a paragraph.	Step 3. Activities that will cause this learning via connections between column A and column B, along with prior learning in this class and prior/current learning in other classes. * _____ • Ask students to tape record their individual answers to questions about topics of interest, transcribe their comments and convert the spoken words into paragraphs. • Have students select their 3 favorite foods and write a paragraph with one separate sentence about each of the favorites. • Have students write the announcements for the school newspaper, using one paragraph per announcement. • Have students write a mini-review of yesterday's school cafeteria lunch, similar to a newspaper food critic's column. • Have students write a mini-review of an extracurricular activity, similar to a newspaper movie critic's article.

Table 3.4   Extreme Teaching: Lesson Plan Design for Paragraph Writing, Part 2

With this lesson, students will make connections between what they know, what they are interested in, what they are good at and *writing a story or report*.

Column A	Column B	Column C
Step 1. What students know, are interested in and/or are good at that relates to this topic: • How to write a paragraph. • Websites, chat rooms, e-mail and other electronic communications of one-page length. • Social notes that students pass to each other. • Completing forms to participate in activities, to apply for a job, to attend an event. • Reading one-page length stories in newspapers or magazines. • Conversations that are equal to one page of dialogue.	Step 2. What students need to learn and know: • How to write a one-page article/story/report.	Step 3. Activities that will cause this learning via connections between column A and column B, along with prior learning in this class and prior/current learning in other classes. * _____ • Have students rewrite stories from 2 or 3 newspapers and/or news magazines to create a one-page article that combines the information from all sources. Remind them to use proper citation methods. • Have 2 students interview each other and use the information from the interview to write a one-page story about each other. • Create a web page for your class, with each student contributing a one-page article. • Select a topic of high interest to students such as a new rule at school. Have students write one-page editorials about the new rule. • Have each student interview a teacher to write a one-page story about the teacher.

Table 3.5   Extreme Teaching: Lesson Plan Design for Reading Comprehension, Part 1

With this lesson, students will make connections between what they know, what they are interested in, what they are good at and *improved reading comprehension.*

Column A	Column B	Column C
Step 1. What students know, are interested in and/or are good at that relates to this topic. • Signs, billboards and advertisements seen, read and understood at stores, malls or along a road. • Words that appear on a television screen. • Website addresses. • Website contents. • Traditional post office mail that is addressed to the student. • Report cards at school. • Rule books and play books that coaches give to athletes. • Newspaper stories about sports and entertainment. • Magazine articles about teenagers' issues and topics.	Step 2. What students need to learn and know: • How to better understand and comprehend what they read.	Step 3. Activities that will cause this learning via connections between column A and column B, along with prior learning in this class and prior/current learning in other classes. * _____ • Have the principal of the school clearly announce over the public address system: "no running in the halls or anyplace else at school at any time. This is necessary for health and safety." Have each student write down the words of that announcement and write an explanation of what it means, why it was announced and what is now required. • Have students take the stories in the school newspaper, read them and write what each story means. They then do this with articles of interest to them from the local community newspaper. • Have students read one paragraph, one page and one chapter in a book and then rewrite or paraphrase it with emphasis on the student using his or her own words to express the meaning of the material. • List only the nouns from a paragraph and ask students to extrapolate the full content and meaning of the paragraph. Then add a list of the verbs to enhance understanding. Then essential prepositions, conjunctions, adverbs and adjectives are added. This could be done with famous documents—the Gettysburg Address, for example—or with common correspondence.

Table 3.6   Extreme Teaching: Lesson Plan Design for Reading Comprehension, Part 2

With this lesson, students will make connections between what they know, what they are interested in, what they are good at and *improved reading comprehension.*

Column A	Column B	Column C
Step 1. What students know, are interested in and/or are good at that relates to this topic:	Step 2. What students need to learn and know:	Step 3. Activities that will cause this learning via connections between column A and column B, along with prior learning in this class and prior/current learning in other classes.
• Comprehending material that they read.	• How to critique, analyze, question and comprehend what they read.	* _____
• Discussing who is best at a sport in professional, college, high school, middle school or neighborhood competition.		• Two state universities play each other in a very important basketball game. Students read pertinent articles the day after the game from the newspaper in each city to compare and contrast content, emphasis, perspective and accuracy.
• Comparing prices of clothes, fast food, cars, entertainment.		• Have students use two print advertisements for two competing products to analyze the claims and the evidence.
• Awareness of bold claims on television infomercials		• Have students watch a 1-minute segment that you have recorded from last night's television news. Then, have them read 3 different versions you have written of the same story these should be at various levels of accuracy and thoroughness. Have students compare and contrast the written materials with each other and with the 1-minute video.
• Critiquing movies they have seen: what was good and why?		
• Analyzing advertisements of new consumer products such as a new soft drink.		• Invite a local car dealer and a banker to talk to students about the reality of buying a car versus what students read in a print advertisement.

Table 3.7 Extreme Teaching: Lesson Plan Design for Causes of Wars, Part 1

With this lesson, students will make connections between what they know, what they are interested in, what they are good at and *causes of wars.*

Column A	Column B	Column C
Step 1. What students know, are interested in and/or are good at that relates to this topic. • Involvement in arguments, misunderstandings and conflicts with friends. • What happens when students gossip about each other, confront each other and then fight. • The penalties used when school rules are broken. • The penalties used when driving and road safety rules are broken. • What happens when people seek revenge. • The importance of safety and security (defense) to make school a safe place.	Step 2. What students need to learn and know: • What causes war between nations and within a nation.	Step 3. Activities that will cause this learning via connections between column A and column B, along with prior learning in this class and prior/current learning in other classes. * _____ • Provide realistic school situations in which gossip, theft, teasing, bullying or cheating led to escalating conflicts that ended in a fight. Explore alternative actions that could have been taken at each level of escalation. Why were those alternatives not taken? • Have students read a U.S. history book's account of the Revolutionary War and contrast that with an account of that event from a book of British history. • Invite guest speakers who participated in wars to give their understanding of what caused the war and what the objectives of the war were. • Have a school counselor speak to a class about similarities and differences in conflicts between students and conflicts between countries. • Use websites, current newspapers, news magazines and journals to list all international wars, current civil wars and the causes of each war, plus the issues/conflicts associated with each war. Ask students: What common causes are found? What atypical causes are found? How do these relate to common causes of conflicts between students at school?

Table 3.8   Extreme Teaching: Lesson Plan Design for Causes of Wars, Part 2

With this lesson, students will make connections between what they know, what they are interested in, what they are good at and *causes of wars.*

Column A	Column B	Column C
Step 1. What students know, are interested in and/or are good at that relates to this topic: • What causes war between nations and within a nation. • How they have dealt with the loss after a friendship ended. • How their community has dealt with recovery following a weather-related disaster or a fire.	Step 2. What students need to learn and know: • Causes of wars and how countries recover after a war.	Step 3. Activities that will cause this learning via connections between column A and column B, along with prior learning in this class and prior/current learning in other classes. * _____ • Have students talk to family members who experienced the effort of the United States to renew normal life after World War II. • Invite fire department officials, Red Cross officials and emergency management officials to speak to students about rescue, recovery and rebuilding efforts after a crisis. • Have students read history books, biographies and autobiographies of people who have overcome difficulties and books about communities and nations that had to rebuild after war. • Create and practice simulation activities for real emergencies such as earthquakes, and think through all recovery work needed after that type of disaster. • Read about the Marshall Plan for Europe after World War II. Create modern "Marshall Plans" that could address current concerns such as diseases or aging infrastructure (roads, sewers, water systems, public buildings including schools).

Table 3.9 Extreme Teaching: Lesson Plan Design for Research, Part 1

With this lesson, students will make connections between what they know, what they are interested in, what they are good at and *doing research for a report.*

Column A	Column B	Column C
Step 1. What students know, are interested in and/or are good at that relates to this topic: • Details about entertainment and entertainers, actors, actresses, musicians, amusement parks, movies, video games. • Statistics about athletes, teams, sports. • How to search on the Internet. • What high school classes to take, what certain teachers require, what school activities to get involved in. • How certain family members will react to particular requests.	Step 2. What students need to learn and know: • How to do research for a report.	Step 3. Activities that will cause this learning via connections between column A and column B, along with prior learning in this class and prior/current learning in other classes. * _____ • Have students use statistics from local football and basketball games to see what the winning team did better. Then have them talk to coaches and players to see if they mention the same reasons and/or other reasons. Have students compare and contrast the insights or conclusions using statistics versus using interviews. • Have students select a favorite hobby, such as skateboarding. Have them search in books, articles, magazines, interviews, stores and other sources to learn how this hobby began, how it has changed and what is likely to happen to it in the near future. • Have students select a career of interest to them. Ask them to interview 5 people who currently do that work to learn how they prepared for their career and what the work is actually like. • Have students select a person from history they want to know more about, and find 4 sources of information about the person. The 4 sources will likely give information that is not identical; ask students what that tells them about research. Have students list the most important facts about the person's life. Why did they select each of those facts? Have them write a short biography of the person, using only 5 of those facts. Ask what the impact is of having to leave out important facts.

Table 3.10 Extreme Teaching: Lesson Plan Design for Research, Part 2

With this lesson, students will make connections between what they know, what they are interested in, what they are good at and *doing research for a report*.

Column A	Column B	Column C
Step 1. What students know, are interested in and/or are good at that relates to this topic: • How to do research for a report. • Having a desired amount of spending money. • Prices of many products. • What they can afford now and what they cannot afford now. • What possessions they would like to have in the future. • How quickly money can be spent, often with little to show for it. • The fact that many prices seem to go up while some go down. • How driving a car is more expensive than anticipated.	Step 2. What students need to learn and know: • Conducting research to select the best practices of money management for a report.	Step 3. Activities that will cause this learning via connections between column A and column B, along with prior learning in this class and prior/current learning in other classes. * _____ • Ask students to keep a complete accounting of every penny they spend during one week and to keep the same record of all income they obtain that week. Now, have them look for ways to honestly, fairly, legally and ethically reduce spending and increase income. • Give students a list of 10 very common consumer products found at grocery stores or department stores. Have them get prices at several different stores for the same 10 items. Compare and contrast results. • Have students collect information from different banks about savings accounts, checking accounts, mortgages and individual retirement accounts. Ask them: What varies from bank to bank and why? • Send a survey to community members, including bankers, asking for guidance about money management. Then, create a bank for students to use at school. • Collect mailings from credit card companies and have students read the fine print. Do math problems to see what happens when credit card bills are not paid promptly. • Have students calculate the total costs over the life of a mortgage

continued

Table 3.10 *(continued)*

Column A	Column B	Column C
		loan for 30 years versus 15 years, each at various interest rates.
		• Have students research all costs associated with owning and maintaining a car.
		• Have students run a concession stand at school extracurricular events and after school each day to apply market research, pricing, promotion, advertising, accounting and money management ideas.

Table 3.11   Extreme Teaching: Lesson Plan Design for Supply and Demand, Part 1

With this lesson, students will make connections between what they know, what they are interested in, what they are good at and *the economic law of supply and demand.*

Column A	Column B	Column C
Step 1. What students know, are interested in and/or are good at that relates to this topic: • Stores' way of charging higher or lower prices for certain products at different times of the year. • Baseball cards or other collectible items that they have traded. • Gasoline prices' variations with international events or decisions, and with different times of the year. • The phenomenon that "When you have a boyfriend every guy wants to go out with you, then when you don't have a boyfriend no guy wants to go out	Step 2. What students need to learn and know: • The economic law of supply and demand.	Step 3. Activities that will cause this learning via connections between column A and column B, along with prior learning in this class and prior/current learning in other classes. * _____ • Invite a retail store manager from a store popular with the students to speak to the class about the law of supply and demand as it impacts the store. • Have students discuss why some athletic events or concerts are sold out even at high ticket prices, while others at higher/equal/lower ticket prices are not sold out. • Get information about the cost of advertising for ½ minute commercials on many different television programs and get rating/share/audience age data for those shows. Discuss the cost/impact of decisions to

continued

Table 3.11 *(continued)*

Column A	Column B	Column C
with you" (actual comment to author by a female teenager).		advertise on different programs, assuming a limited advertising budget.
• The fact that when parents/guardians demand good grades and good grades are supplied, beneficial results can occur; with a low supply of good grades, problems occur.		• Have students consider the following scenario: The soft drink price at school increases. What impact does that have on sales?
		• Give students the following scenario: One school group had a car wash and charged $5 per car. Another group provided a free car wash but took donations. The second group actually took in more money. How could supply and demand help explain this?

Table 3.12 Extreme Teaching: Lesson Plan Design for Supply and Demand, Part 2

With this lesson, students will make connections between what they know, what they are interested in, what they are good at and *the economic law of supply and demand.*

Column A	Column B	Column C
Step 1. What students know, are interested in and/or are good at that relates to this topic: • The economic law of supply and demand. • The fact that if they watch too much television and do not finish their homework, they get in trouble. • The fact that if they take a full schedule of hard classes they'll have more homework and less free time, but they'll have a stronger foundation for college. • The fact that if they ask one person to a dance they can't ask another person to the dance. • The fact that if they go with the group to the game out of town and get home after their curfew, they can't go to any more games.	Step 2. What students need to learn and know: • The economic concepts of supply and demand and of opportunity cost.	Step 3. Activities that will cause this learning via connections between column A and column B, along with prior learning in this class and prior/current learning in other classes. * _____ • Create a catalogue of products that students like. Give each student an amount of play money/credit. Have the students explain their purchases or their decision to keep money in terms of opportunity cost. • Have the local zoning commission leader talk to students about opportunity costs related to land. • Have students keep a log for one week of how they use their free time each week. Have them explain their time use decisions in term of opportunity cost. • Have students research their options for college, military service, technical/trade school or a job right out of high school. Looking at short-term and long-term opportunity costs, which option works best for each student and why?

Table 3.13   Extreme Teaching: Lesson Plan Design for Analyzing Data, Part 1

With this lesson, students will make connections between what they know, what they are interested in, what they are good at and *analyzing data*.

Column A	*Column B*	*Column C*
Step 1. What students know, are interested in and/or are good at that relates to this topic:	Step 2. What students need to learn and know: • How to analyze data.	Step 3. Activities that will cause this learning via connections between column A and column B, along with prior learning in this class and prior/current learning in other classes. * _____
• Who won a sports event based on the score alone.		
• What grades have to be made to maintain eligibility for athletes or for car insurance discounts.		• Give the students a collection of weather information from all parts of the country and have them predict tomorrow's weather based on the data.
• What team will win the Super Bowl or the World Series or the NCAA March Madness tournament based on data from past performance.		• Give the students a sample monthly checking account statement with cancelled checks. Have them balance the checkbook and evaluate how the person is managing his or her checking account.
• The grade they will make in science class this year, based on the grades they've always made in science classes before.		• Get information about car sales in the United States for the past 10 years. Have students identify trends, constants and innovations. Have them predict the sales for the next year and give reasons for their predictions.
• Where to buy gasoline for less money.		• Use census data to identify demographic changes during the past 5 decades.
• What a SAT or ACT score means.		• Use the stock market results from the newspaper to evaluate how the stocks of 10 well-known companies have done in the past year.
		• Give students all of their grades from a class for the year and have them evaluate why they have their current grade. What roles did homework, tests, papers, projects and class participation play in the overall grade? What should they do to improve a bad grade or to keep a good grade?

Table 3.14   Extreme Teaching: Lesson Plan Design for Analyzing Data, Part 2

With this lesson, students will make connections between what they know, what they are interested in, what they are good at and *analyzing data.*

Column A	Column B	Column C
Step 1. What students know, are interested in and/or are good at that relates to this topic: • How to analyze data. • What they have heard from friends and family about various jobs. • Oral presentations made in classes at school or at activities other than school. • Prior experience with applications and/or interviews. • Forms that students have filled out for school data sheets that may be similar to some job applications. • Some conferences with teachers, principals and coaches that may have been similar to job interviews.	Step 2. What students need to learn and know: • How to analyze data when applying for a job and interviewing for a job.	Step 3. Activities that will cause this learning via connections between column A and column B, along with prior learning in this class and prior/current learning in other classes. * _____ • Get actual job applications for students to fill out. • Have a local employer speak to a class about what makes for a successful job application and interview. • Invite a local fast food restaurant manager to conduct real job interviews with interested students who could get a job right on the spot. • Have students report their findings from Internet searches of websites that relate to jobs.

Table 3.15　Extreme Teaching: Lesson Plan Design for States and Capitals, Part 1

With this lesson, students will make connections between what they know, what they are interested in, what they are good at and *locating each of the fifty states on a map.*

Column A	Column B	Column C
Step 1. What students know, are interested in and/or are good at that relates to this topic: • The state in which they live. • Some/all of the states that border their state. • Other states where they have relatives or friends. • Other states where they have lived or visited. • Puzzles and trivia games. • Television—game/information shows. • Major cities, events or attractions in some states. • How to use computer software programs about geography. • Car license plates from various states.	Step 2. What students need to learn and know: • The location of each of the 50 states on a map.	Step 3. Activities that will cause this learning via connections between column A and column B, along with prior learning in this class and prior/current learning in other classes. *　_____ • Use an old-fashioned wood or cardboard puzzle map of the United States. Let each student assemble the puzzle. Then use a computer software program that does the same puzzle on the screen. • Play a U.S. geography trivia game. Students answer questions about geography and locate the state that relates to the question/answer on a large map, which everyone can see. • Calculate the distance from where the students live to each of the other states. Group and identify states by distance categories such as 0–500 miles away, 501–1,000 miles away, etc. • Have students identify something they know about each state and put their identifying facts on a map showing each of the states. • Have students make/use old-fashioned flash cards with the name of a state on one side and a drawing of the state on the other side. • Frequently have students identify states on a U.S. map. Have students monitor their progress as they work toward knowing all 50 states.

continued

Table 3.15 *(continued)*

Column A	Column B	Column C
		• Invite the principal to compete with the students in a "Name that State" game show. • Have spelling tests on the names of the states.

Table 3.16 Extreme Teaching: Lesson Plan Design for States and Capitals, Part 2

With this lesson, students will make connections between what they know, what they are interested in, what they are good at and *state capitals*.

Column A	Column B	Column C
Step 1. What students know, are interested in and/or are good at that relates to this topic: • The location of each of the 50 states on a map. • The capital of their home state. • Capitals they have visited or have relatives and friends living in. • Television game shows where questions about state capitals are used. • Keeping score and/or trying to beat a time limit.	Step 2. What students need to learn and know: • The capital of each state.	Step 3. Activities that will cause this learning via connections between column A and column B, along with prior learning in this class and prior/current learning in other classes. * _____ • Have students write or e-mail students in the capital of each state. • Students can visit the tourism information website for each state and learn about the capital, location, history and current facts. • Use/make old-fashioned flash cards with the state name on one side and the state capital name on the other. • Have students research each state's history to see if other cities ever served as capital, why the current capital was chosen and any historical significance or meaning of the name of the capital city. • Have a 1-minute drill to see which students can name all 50 state capitals in 1 minute.

Table 3.17   Extreme Teaching: Lesson Plan Design for Multiplication

With this lesson, students will make connections between what they know, what they are interested in, what they are good at and *the multiplication table through 12 x 12.*

Column A	Column B	Column C
Step 1. What students know, are interested in and/or are good at that relates to this topic: • Using numbers in daily activities such as telling time, counting change after a purchase, keeping score in a game or taking one's temperature when ill. • Buying and using gasoline—how many gallons can I afford; how many miles will I get from these gallons. • Calculating sports statistics, such as points scored from 2-point shots versus 3-point shots in a basketball game. • Ordering pizza for a group of people: 16 people, 3 slices of pizza per person equals how many pizzas to order?	Step 2. What students need to learn and know: • The multiplication table through 12 x 12	Step 3. Activities that will cause this learning via connections between column A and column B, along with prior learning in this class and prior/current learning in other classes. * _____ • Give students a 144-box grid with the numbers 1–12 across the top and 1–12 going down the left side. Have them multiply the numbers to fill in each of the 144 boxes. Then have them look for patterns in the numbers. • Create a grocery store shopping activity in which sizes, prices and brands are compared and contrasted using math. • Use old-fashioned flash cards for drill and practice. • Use new-fashioned computer software for drill and practice. • Use basketball game statistics to calculate points scored by teams based on free throws, 2-point shots and 3-point shots. Ask students: What do these statistics suggest was most important to winning the game? • Ask students: If 8 students each eat 4 slices of pizza, how many slices were eaten? If 12 students have 12 pennies each, how many total pennies are there? Create a word problem for each multiplication pair of numbers in the 12 by 12 grid.

Table 3.18   Extreme Teaching: Lesson Plan Design for Multiplication and Division

With this lesson, students will make connections between what they know, what they are interested in, what they are good at and *division*

Column A	Column B	Column C
Step 1. What students know, are interested in and/or are good at that relates to this topic: • The multiplication tables through 12 x 12. • The concept that when a pizza is sliced into 8 slices, it's being divided. • The fact that when they take their allowance or paychecks and budget their money for each day, they are dividing. • The fact that when a school has 8 class periods per day, it has divided the school day into separate classes for separate subjects. • The fact that sporting events are divided into quarters or halves or periods. • How a dollar can be divided into various amounts of change from 100 pennies to two half-dollar coins.	Step 2. What students need to learn and know: • That division is the opposite of multiplication.	Step 3. Activities that will cause this learning via connections between column A and column B, along with prior learning in this class and prior/current learning in other classes. * _____ • Have students create poems or songs or raps with lyrics such as "36 divided by 12 is 3/36 divided by 9 is 4 but there is still one more/36 divided by 6 is 6/ now it all clicks cause 6 times 6 is 36." • Use 8-ounce cups of water to fill a pitcher with 64 ounces of water. Then divide the 64 ounces into two 32-ounce bottles, four 16-ounce bottles and eight 8-ounce bottles or cups. • Use word problems that relate to money, such as "Jason was paid $30 for 4 hours of work. How much was he paid per hour? How many more hours does he need to work to make $45 more?" • Use sports problems such as the following: A football team scored 28 points, with equal points in the first and fourth quarters and no points in the second or third quarters. How many points did they score in the 1st quarter? In the 2nd quarter?

Table 3.19 Extreme Teaching: Lesson Plan Design for Music, Part 1

With this lesson, students will make connections between what they know, what they are interested in, what they are good at and *identifying uses of music in different cultures.*

Column A	Column B	Column C
Step 1. What students know, are interested in and/or are good at that relates to this topic:	Step 2. What students need to learn and know:	Step 3. Activities that will cause this learning via connections between column A and column B, along with prior learning in this class and prior/current learning in other classes.
• The types of music they like, listen to or buy.	• How to identify uses of music in different cultures.	* _____
• The occasions when they play music.		• Invite local residents of varying ethnic heritages to present information about and examples of music from their homelands.
• Events in their society when music is used—weddings, athletic events, television commercials, church services, funerals, school pep rallies.		• As a class, listen to music of the United States from different time periods in our history.
• Some students know how to play a musical instrument and may have performed at various events.		• Using ordinary materials at school or home, have students make simple musical instruments. Compare/contrast these with the instruments of ancient civilizations and how they were made.
• The fact that different radio stations play different types of music.		• Use websites to listen to music from around the world and compare/contrast it with American music.
		• Interview people of different age groups to learn of various musical preferences and uses.
		• Have students use books, audiotapes, videotapes and publications to research music from different cultures.
		• If your community has ethnic/cultural festivals, videotape musical presentations from the festivals.
		• Have students create music videos using different types of music from various cultures.

Table 3.20   Extreme Teaching: Lesson Plan Design for Music, Part 2

With this lesson, students will make connections between what they know, what they are interested in, what they are good at and *identifying uses of music in different cultures.*

Column A	Column B	Column C
Step 1. What students know, are interested in and/or are good at that relates to this topic: • Different uses of music in various cultures. • The best places to buy music CDs. • The best Internet sites for music information or webcasts of music. • The best concerts to attend. • Currently popular musicians. • The cost of CDs, CD players, car music systems, concerts and concert souvenirs. • Advertisements or movies that feature popular musicians. • The best local radio stations.	Step 2. What students need to learn and know: • How the music business in different cultures operates as a case study in economics.	Step 3. Activities that will cause this learning via connections between column A and column B, along with prior learning in this class and prior/current learning in other classes. * _____ • Have students collect comparison price information about CDs, CD players and car music systems from various local retailers. • Invite the managers of a local radio station and a local music store to speak to the class. • Invite the manager of a big arena that hosts large concerts to visit class or to speak to the class via new technology (speakerphone, video conference or e-mail). • Have students get information from the websites of popular musicians. Have them critique the advertising methods used to appeal to teenagers to buy CDs and to attend concerts. • Have students evaluate how celebrity musicians influence people to buy the products they endorse. • Have students research the development of record players, radios, 8-track tapes, cassette tapes and CDs. Ask students: What human creative forces, technology changes and business opportunities have inspired the development of new music systems for consumers to have at home or in cars? • Discuss local noise ordinances that govern the

continued

Table 3.20 *(continued)*

Column A	Column B	Column C
		sound levels of music played in cars, at residential parties or at other community locations. What interest does the music industry have in these laws?

Table 3.21   Extreme Teaching: Lesson Plan Design for Architecture, Part 1

With this lesson, students will make connections between what they know, what they are interested in, what they are good at and *how/why pyramids were built in ancient Egypt*.

Column A	Column B	Column C
Step 1. What students know, are interested in and/or are good at that relates to this topic: • How they built forts, castles, sand box structures and other "buildings" with toys when they were children. • Some math concepts that relate to squares, triangles and measurements. • Some science concepts that relate to force, mass and leverage. • Some information about, or at least pictures of, Egyptian pyramids. • Some awareness of current burial and funeral processes. • Some understanding of ceremonial occasions and the tributes for leading citizens in a society during their lives and at their deaths.	Step 2. What students need to learn and know: • How/why pyramids were built in ancient Egypt.	Step 3. Activities that will cause this learning via connections between column A and column B, along with prior learning in this class and prior/current learning in other classes. * _____ • Have students build a pyramid using various materials such as bricks, concrete blocks, sugar cubes, toy blocks, cardboard or wood. Require a design prior to construction and an explanation for each element of the design. • Have students search the Internet for information, pictures, theories and facts about the pyramids. • Invite a local college professor or other local resident who has visited the pyramids to speak to the students. • Have students create a new, modern amusement park called Pyramid Park. Everything— rides, restaurants, souvenirs, uniforms for employees—must relate to ancient Egypt. • Have students compare/ contrast an Egyptian pharaoh's job with that of the president of the United States. Ask students: why are no pyramids built for presidents?

continued

Table 3.21 *(continued)*

Column A	Column B	Column C
		• Have students conduct imaginary interviews with laborers who worked for many years on pyramid building.
		• Have students create an episode of a television program called "Pyramid Improvement," which deals with how/why pyramids were built and how they have eroded over the years, plus ideas for helping to maintain and preserve the pyramids.

Table 3.22 Extreme Teaching: Lesson Plan Design for Architecture, Part 2

With this lesson, students will make connections between what they know, what they are interested in, what they are good at and *how architecture can provide insights into history*.

Column A	Column B	Column C
Step 1. What students know, are interested in and/or are good at that relates to this topic: • How/why pyramids were built in Egypt. • The design of buildings they are familiar with—home, school, stores, churches and sports facilities. • Different styles of architecture in older versus newer parts of their community. • What design in fashion or in cars appeals to them, and how those designs relate to the function of clothes or cars. • What pictures and images in video games are most convincing.	Step 2. What students need to learn and know: • What architecture can tell about the history of people and places.	Step 3. Activities that will cause this learning via connections between column A and column B, along with prior learning in this class and prior/current learning in other classes. * _____ • Have students use computer-assisted design software to create architectural concepts and show how their design forms relate to the intended functions of the structures. • Through pictures, videos, websites, journals and tourism brochures, have students "travel" in time or in distance to evaluate houses, schools, factories, public buildings and other buildings to assess what the buildings reveal about the lifestyle, priorities, values and technology of different eras. • Visit nearby houses built from various times during the past century or earlier. Have students

continued

Table 3.22 *(continued)*

Column A	Column B	Column C
		each write a story about how life was impacted by the house's design, stability and comfort.

Table 3.23   Extreme Teaching: Lesson Plan Design for Government, Part 1

With this lesson, students will make connections between what they know, what they are interested in, what they are good at and *how laws are made by the U.S. government.*

Column A	Column B	Column C
Step 1. What students know, are interested in and/or are good at that relates to this topic: • Rules at home and how they are made. • Unwritten, but still followed, rules among friends and how they are made. • Rules in classrooms at school and how they are made. • Rules for the entire school and some awareness of how they are made. • Local traffic/driving laws. • Juvenile justice laws. • Rules of sports and games.	Step 2. What students need to learn and know: • How the U.S. government makes laws. • Legislative branch of the government. • Executive branch of the government.	Step 3. Activities that will cause this learning via connections between column A and column B, along with prior learning in this class and prior/current learning in other classes. * _____ • Have students write a short paper telling what they know about the process used to make a law in our national government. Compile their knowledge into one summary and their misunderstandings into another summary. Confirm what was right and correct what was wrong. • Edit video clips of the president, senators and representatives at news conferences giving thoughts about pending legislation. Help students separate fact, opinion, posturing, "spin," leadership and playing politics. • List each step in the process of a bill becoming a law, but put these steps in the wrong order. Have students work individually, then in small groups to correct the sequence. See how accurate each individual was and how accurate each group was. • Divide the class into senators, representatives and a president. Have them conduct a mock session of Congress to debate bills and to send those approved to the president for signature, veto or

continued

Table 3.23 *(continued)*

Column A	Column B	Column C
		inaction. Send the approved bills to the actual U.S. senators and the U.S. representatives of the students to ask for formal congressional consideration of their ideas. Videotape the deliberations of the "Senate" and "House of Representatives" and their committees so students can critique their own work.

Table 3.24   Extreme Teaching: Lesson Plan Design for Government, Part 2

With this lesson, students will make connections between what they know, what they are interested in, what they are good at and *how laws are made by the U.S. government.*

Column A	Column B	Column C
Step 1. What students know, are interested in and/or are good at that relates to this topic: • How laws are made by the U.S. government. • Legislative branch of our government. • Executive branch of our government. • Times when one adult has given them a certain instruction and then a higher-ranking adult gave a different instruction. • Making plans for weekend activities with friends and then being told of a mandatory family event to attend. • Being hired for a part-time job and then being laid off after a short time (e.g., when a new owner of the company decided to close your location).	Step 2. What students need to learn and know: • How the U.S. Supreme Court can declare a law to be unconstitutional.	Step 3. Activities that will cause this learning via connections between column A and column B, along with prior learning in this class and prior/current learning in other classes. * _____ • Invite 9 faculty and staff members plus 2 local lawyers to present a Supreme Court hearing of a case involving one of the bills the students approved and the student president signed into law in part 1 of this lesson. Have each student predict the court's decision by writing an official majority decision of the court. Compare/contrast predictions with the mock court's actual decision. • Read real Supreme Court cases of interest to students. One good choice might be *Tinker vs. Des Moines,* when the issue was whether wearing armbands at school is protected by the First Amendment. • Have students research the actual cases currently being

continued

Table 3.24   *(continued)*

Column A	Column B	Column C
		heard by the U.S. Supreme Court, monitor the argument before the court and read the opinion of the court when it is issued.

Jason was quite confident that a correct understanding of the idea of Extreme Teaching combined with an effective implementation of Extreme Teaching could symbiotically impact a classroom by causing a new deep quality of learning and a large quantity of learning by students while also creating new career satisfaction for teachers. Still, Jason thought it would be wise to keep Paula Hammisch informed, to seek her input along the way and to gain her support for Extreme Teaching. So, before creating more Extreme Teaching lesson plans, Jason decided to share the work he had done with Paula Hammisch.

Jason sent Paula the 24 lesson plans presented above. He asked her to read them and to offer her perspective on them and on the Extreme Teaching idea. Jason reminded Paula that the essential idea of Extreme Teaching is to build upon what students know, are interested in and/or are good at as a foundation for connections with what students need to know. He also reminded Paula that the implementation of Extreme Teaching would include a variety of classroom activities that range from the old-fashioned use of paper flash cards to use of the newest, fastest, most compelling technology. Jason eagerly awaited a response from Paula. The response came quickly, but it also came in a surprising form. Paula visited Jason after school two days following her receipt of the lesson plans. They met in Jason's classroom a few minutes after he finished an after-school tutoring session with several students who were doing extra credit work and enrichment work. (These were students who were eager to learn more and who voluntarily stayed after school one day per week to work with Mr. Prather).

> Paula: Jason, so good to see you. Thanks for taking the time to meet with me. Thanks also for all the work you're doing for our school district. Your Extreme Teaching ideas are very—well, very interesting to me.

Jason: Come on, Paula, interesting means nothing. Let's get to the point. Nobody has time to waste, and we know each other well enough to skip the diplomacy and speak bluntly.

Paula: OK, I'll be blunt. Jason, I expected something from you that would be, well, that would be really complicated. I thought you would recommend—oh, what's the word?—a new paradigm or a new philosophy. I expected the typical education innovation and reform that includes lots of new policies and procedures plus lots of new equipment or materials. I certainly thought that you would include articles from professional journals and other research to build the case for your recommendation. You know that superintendents and school boards often want to see results from other places where a new idea was used before they give it serious thought. Plus, the media and the community members need to be convinced.

So, Jason, if I read your materials correctly, you're not asking for money or policies or laws or more staff. You just propose a different way of teaching as the solution for the low test scores in our school district. That's it, right? Just a different way of teaching that you say has worked well with your students for the past two years? Help me understand this, please.

Jason: Paula, you're a teacher at heart. You're an educator. Don't let the big bureaucracy change you into a clerk or a paper pusher. Our job is to cause learning, not to write different policies or to lobby for more money. What matters most out of all the factors and variables that educators can control is what happens in the classroom. Teaching, Paula, teaching is the essence of what we do. I'll put great teaching up against anything and everything else that schools can provide. Give our students great teaching and they will learn. After they learn, they will do well on any test. It's all about teaching, which means it's all about causing learning.

If you prefer policies and laws, tax increases and grant applications, procedures and bigger bureaucracies, then we really disagree on what matters most in school. But if your goal is to improve student learning, then the most important action to take is to improve the effectiveness of teaching. If that sounds less complicated than the recommendation you expected, then it's a reminder that sometimes education reformers or educators themselves can overlook the most obvious and important ideas and solutions. Don't search for the bureaucratic, the complex, the expensive when the human, the simple, the available will do. School is all about teaching and learning. School is all about teachers teaching in ways that cause students to learn. Teaching and learning are so basic that perhaps my method seems shocking or extreme, which is another reason to call the concept Extreme Teaching. Now, what part of that thinking doesn't make sense?

Paula: It does make sense. Great teaching and great learning have made sense forever. When Socrates used his brilliant sequence of increasingly precise and powerful questions, he was connecting what students knew with what they needed to learn. Socrates used his own version of Extreme Teaching. It worked then and maybe it could work now. Jesus Christ used parables to teach, and those simple stories connected the real life of his students with the big ideas he was teaching. So, Jesus was another extreme teacher. I can't argue too much with your ideas, Jason, if you advocate a teaching concept that Socrates and Jesus Christ endorsed; however, I can debate whether your Extreme Teaching approach is all our school district needs to do to reach our test score goals. That's my real concern, Jason. I know you're a great teacher. I know the methods you use get results. We hired that student teacher who worked with you last year, and she's the best first-year teacher I've ever seen. You know what you're doing, but can I really go to the superintendent and the school board and simply say, "It's easy. We teach better and then we cause more learning by students and then test scores go up, that's it."

Jason: Paula, come on, where's your courage and sense of adventure and enthusiasm? You haven't become a bureaucrat, have you? You're still in this for students, right? You aren't in this for meetings and task forces and policies and systems, are you?

Paula: The students are my priority. That's why I have to caution you: you dream big dreams, Jason. Those are wonderful dreams, but making big dreams happen in a school district can mean getting the big bureaucracy to create new policies, hire new staff members, reorganize the chain of command, set up a new evaluation system, review all budgets and the budget system. Plus it means saying no to other big dreams because of limitations on money, on time people have, on how much change can happen at once, on the political realities of the day, on the community priorities, on the labor market, on current employees and their morale. Sure, great ideas deserve great support, but we can't do everything, and what we can do has to be according to priorities. The top priority in this school district right now is to substantially increase test scores across all grade levels. Your idea of Extreme Teaching and any other idea from any other person must show that it can increase test scores. Do you have that proof?

Jason: I'll get the proof. I've used the Extreme Teaching method for two years. I'll analyze how my students did on the state tests. I'll compare and contrast students I taught with students I didn't teach. I'll show you the facts, and those facts will be the reality check for Extreme Teaching.

I'm also going to keep creating recommendations for our think group. I think the facts will support Extreme Teaching, so while I get the facts I'll also take the risk of making more Extreme Teaching lesson ideas. That way, when the facts are available I'll also have a complete set of lesson plans to show our think group how the method can be used by any teacher with any topic and any group of students. So, you've read the materials I've written so far. Advise me. What's good? What needs to improve?

Paula: Get real about working conditions. Bring the dream down to the reality of the typical teacher's work schedule and work ethic and work perspective. Not every teacher has the time or the imagination to see teaching as you see it or to do teaching as you do it.

Jason: Maybe, but if there is a way to teach that creates more student success and more career satisfaction for teachers, wouldn't that be of interest to people?

Paula: Jason, teaching is complicated, demanding, difficult, tiring and hard, and people in teaching are not easily convinced that one simple idea will solve the problems. What makes you so confident about Extreme Teaching? You and I both know that far too often educators are asked or told to make major changes in what they do at school because of some new idea that will supposedly fix all the problems. We change from one method of teaching reading to another method, and then we go back to the original method. We attend some seminar or workshop or training session and hear about the latest cure-all, sure-fire, can't-miss, never-fail solution, but before we get it implemented at our schools we hear that the first schools to use the new plan have quit using it due to poor results. Teachers want their students to learn, but we've become cautious or skeptical of some new ideas because we've watched so many education trends, fads and panaceas come and go. So, Jason, how do you address all of those concerns?

Jason: You make a lot of sense, Paula. I can see why our district selected you as assistant superintendent. I'll address your concerns one step at a time. The first step was to present the Extreme Teaching lesson plan ideas to you and to get your evaluation of that teaching concept and method. I'll use your guidance to improve the extreme lesson plan process. Then, for step two, you and I should meet with our think group to present the Extreme Teaching idea, concept, design, system and method. With their input, I'll make more improvements. Step three is when I will make the final presentation of Extreme Teaching to you and to our think group. If that goes well, we'll present Extreme Teaching to the superintendent. Then this recommendation would be communicated to the school board, the community and the school district employees—teachers especially. We'd give them an implementation plan so everyone could learn to use Extreme Teaching and so everyone would know how to introduce students to Extreme Teaching, how to measure results and how to determine the success or failure of Extreme Teaching.

Paula: OK. That sequence could work, and our think group expects you to create the draft of our group recommendation, so let's keep going. You asked for my input. Here goes: I'd actually encourage you to think bigger. Your system seeks to connect what students know, are interested in or are good at with what they need to learn. Well, if you need me to learn fractions, you hope that I'm aware of pizza slices so you can show me that if I eat one slice out of a pizza that has seven slices left; it means I ate one-eighth of the pizza. But let's imagine that pizza slices and fractions just don't connect for me, but that I love to read. So, I have a book of 12 chapters. Have I read $\frac{1}{12}$ or $\frac{1}{3}$ of the book? Based on chapters, yes. Based on pages, maybe not. Were all chapters the same length in pages? Were the chapters I've read longer or shorter or the same as most chapters? If I've read 50 pages out of 175 pages in the book, that is $\frac{50}{175}$ or $\frac{2}{7}$. Is this the same as $\frac{1}{3}$ or not? So, even if what I know, am interested in or am good at does not seem to directly apply to what the teacher needs me to learn, there can still be some connections found and used.

Jason: Great idea! You might be the most extreme teacher of all. Maybe anything a student knows, is good at or is interested in can, in some creative or useful or even very direct way, set up thinking and learning connections with what needs to be learned. Wonderful advice, Paula. Anything else?

Paula: Yes. Think of reality in the classrooms, Jason. Teachers are told to effectively educate groups of students with vast ranges of academic preparation, intellectual skills and commitment to school. Teaching is already more demanding work than ever, yet we continue to demand more and more from teachers. Extreme Teaching is a fascinating idea, but it has to be a feasible, practical, realistic idea that works on Monday morning in any classroom if you want to see it go anywhere.

Jason: True. True. Very True. OK. In a week I'll have more material for you to review. Then we can meet with our think group. Thanks so much!

Paula: Thanks for your work. You and I agree—teaching effectively is vital. Teaching that causes learning, as you always say, is the bottom line. Just remember, we have to increase test scores. I know, I know. When students are taught so they are learning more and are learning better, the test scores should go up. Still, the political reality is that test scores must improve. Keep dreaming big and thinking big, but keep one foot on the ground so you're in touch with teacher reality, student reality, school board reality and political reality. I'll be eager to hear from you in a week. Let's just plan to meet one week from today in your classroom. See you then.

Jason's memory raced to his college days, which were spent at a small liberal arts college. His four years of college classes ranged from political science to physical science, from anthropology to theater, from French to literature, from philosophy to constitutional law, from history of religion to history of the United States, from western political theory to modern international relations. In the proper liberal arts tradition, Jason studied the dynamic breadth of human knowledge while also earning certification to be a teacher. Jason's college, however, was a pioneer of the approach that requires the aspiring teacher to major in and master the subject area he or she will teach, to gain a breadth of knowledge in and of other subjects plus to take the courses and to complete the student teacher training required by the state teacher certification agency. Jason's college knew that all knowledge is connected, is contiguous and is overlapping and that great teaching is enhanced when a teacher has studied the breadth and width of human knowledge.

Jason now reached a "stop the presses" moment, an "a-ha" moment, a moment that made him say "eureka," which he knew comes from a Greek word that means "I have found it." A liberal arts education ideally shows connections between different academic subjects. A liberal arts education that is most meaningful for students of any age would also show and make the connections within all subjects, categories and topics taught at school plus the connections between those subjects, categories and topics and everything or anything that students already know, already are good at or already are interested in. All pieces of information, all units of knowledge, all measures of understanding, all topics of interest, all previous experience, all prior learning, all acquired talents or skills could connect with and be a foundation for new learning. Plus, that connection could provide a reason to learn, a motivation to study, an inspiration to do homework and a fascination with school that leads to commitment from students and rewarding, challenging, meaningful career experiences for teachers. Wow!

Jason paused to evaluate this new insight. His college professors very rarely showed connections between one subject and another. In theater class he and his fellow students studied some theater history, but they did not connect it with other history or with literature and art and economics or politics. In comparative religion they studied religious ideas and systems but not any connection with literature, politics or sociology. Each class they took in college pretty much stood alone. The classes in one's major area did have some limited similarity in vocabulary, research base or important authors, but even in each major area many more connections could have been made. They took their classes each semester and, after four years of that process, the entire collection of classes was deemed to be a college education and they were confirmed as graduates.

Now, 13 years later, Jason can see how religion, anthropology, French, theater, government, economics, literature and the rest do fit together, do connect and do relate, but that harmony of or symphony of ideas was not an emphasis, a teaching tool or a learning priority in college. It seemed so obvious to him now that all knowledge, all learning, all experience, all teaching, all education can fit together, but the common reality is that knowledge, learning, experience, teaching and education get categorized and separated. The result of the categorization and separation is that learning often becomes a disjointed, multidirectional, almost random process. Show students how the pieces of knowledge they already have fit with the pieces of knowledge they need to acquire, and it suddenly becomes important and possible, fascinating and worthwhile to complete the puzzle.

The sample lesson plan designs that Jason had completed were a good start toward showing other teachers the logical sequence of Extreme Teaching. Connections should also be made with prior learning in all classes; however, with Paula's guidance and with Jason's reflection on that guidance, a massive mental merger of any or all past learning could be used as a foundation for, a connection with and a motivation toward new learning. With that in mind, Jason needed to know more about what students have already learned, are already interested in, and/or are already good at. To get that information, all he had to do was ask students. During the next two school days, Jason had his students complete a very short survey about their interests, their talents, their hobbies, their skills, their expertise, their academic achievements, facts they know, ideas they understand and knowledge they have mastered.

Jason went one step further. He asked what they would like to become talented in, interested in, skilled in, expert in, knowledgeable about, understanding of, informed about and learned about. Jason reflected on the word *learned* which, as an adjective, meant to have obtained much learning or to demonstrate much learning. He realized that the verb *learned* was commonly used in school, but the adjective *learned* was rarely, if ever, used. Why? Did commonly used words such as *scholarly* or *smart*, *intelligent* or *gifted*, fully communicate the potent meaning of "a person who has become or who is becoming learned?" Anyway, Jason's survey results were fascinating to him. He organized the results from his high school students into categories based on how the questions were asked of the students and based on the time frame: whether the learning was already accomplished or the student would like to accomplish it in the future. (The survey results are shown in table 3.25.) Jason would use these results to help him create more Extreme Teaching lessons to use in his classes and to show the district's think group.

Included in Jason's list are things he was told by students in the survey and in some conversations before school, at lunch and after school. Jason noticed that some answers from some students were worded differently but expressed similar thoughts. Some comments were amusing, some were practical, some were troubling, but all were genuine, all were real, all were important, all were revealing and all were worth

Table 3.25   Student Survey Results

continued

Interests

Jason made it clear that topics listed here and in other categories had to be proper, honorable, legal, ethical interests.

Already Interested in		Would Like to Become Interested in
Sports	Volunteer work	Saving money
Food	Music	Mountain climbing
Dating	Movies	The stock market
Skateboarding	Cars	A career
Church	Making money	Scuba diving
Computers	Reading	Architecture
College	Foreign cultures	Space travel
Concerts	Video games	World peace
The Internet	Fashion	Entrepreneurism
Ice skating	Dancing	
The environment	Surfboards	
The military		

Talents

Already Talented in		Would Like to Become Talented in
Cooking	Sewing	Playing a musical instrument
Landscaping	Drawing	Running a marathon
Singing	Athletics	Making good grades
Acting	Writing stories	Planning good parties
Repairing cars	Improving my memory	Changing my car's oil
Saving money	Creativity	Being on time
Making people laugh	Gardening	Telling a joke well
Working with animals	Baby-sitting	Construction work

Hobbies

Already a Hobby		Would Like This to Become a Hobby
Karate	Camping	Bicycle repair
Old movies	Cake decorating	Car repair
Travel	Archeology	Working with wood
Coin collecting	Autograph collecting	Reading
Mountain biking	Rollerblading	Starting a band
Playing cards	Trivia	Volunteering with a charity
Playing board games	Watching television	Political campaigns
Listen to music	Going to the mall	Cooking
Going into caves	Video games	Sports
Hunting	Photography	Fishing
Bowling		

Table 3.25   *(continued)*

<u>*Skills*</u>

Already Skilled in	*Would Like This to Become Skilled in*
Speaking Spanish	Stopping computer viruses
Speaking French	Flying a plane
Writing computer programs	Parachuting
Calligraphy	Making music videos
Sports	Driving a truck
Hunting	Training horses
Dog training	Radio announcing
Writing music	Television broadcasting
Teaching adults to use the Internet	Preaching
Riding and grooming horses	Running a 4-minute mile
Painting	Being a camp counselor

<u>*Expertise*</u>

Already an Expert in	*Would Like This to Become an Expert in*
Chess	Playing guitar
Delivering pizza (it's my job)	The card game of bridge
Calculus	Golf
Word processing	Tennis
Farming (grew up with it)	Saving money
Raising animals	Car maintenance
Baby-sitting	Doing tax returns
Yard work	Managing a restaurant
Using tools	Designing computer software
Acting and modeling	Designing and building computers
Using the Internet	Archery
Helping at vacation Bible school	Sailing boats

<u>*Academic* *Achievements*</u>

Already Achieved	*Would Like to Achieve*
Straight A grades	Understanding classic literature
Doing proofs in geometry	A college scholarship
Learning a new language	Take vocational school classes
Passing calculus	Tutoring younger students
Passing 9th grade	Turning in all homework
Reading books by Charles Dickens	Passing chemistry
Best project at vocational school	Graduating from high school early
Getting out of middle school	Avoiding summer school
Memorizing the Gettysburg Address	

continued

Table 3.25 *(continued)*

Facts Known

Already Know	Would Like to Know
The multiplication table	The best age to get married
$A^2 + B^2 = C^2$	What job pays the most
93 million miles to the sun from Earth	What career I should select
1492—Columbus	The best summer job
How a bill becomes a law	How much to study to pass a test
What pyramids were built for	What makes an airplane fly
The 7 continents	How to apply for colleges
The 50 states and each capital	How to not get grounded
Who wrote the Iliad and the Odyssey	What it costs to have a car
$F = ma$	1 mile = how many feet
A meter is longer than a yard	Equations for converting Celsius and Fahrenheit

Ideas Understood

Already Understand	Would Like to Understand
School is boring	Why parents and teenagers argue
Work is hard	Why my little brothers and sisters bother me
Time flies on weekends	What causes divorce
Supply and demand	Why people are mean
Pollution problems can be prevented	Why teachers who hate school are teachers
Money talks	Why athletes get scholarships
Drunk driving kills people	How to end a romance and still be friends
Drugs are stupid	Why middle school needed to be 3 years
It hurts when friends lie about you	Why high school needs to be 4 years
Schools treat athletes better than scholars	How to pick whom to date
Some teachers really like students	Why some teachers really don't like students
The 10 Commandments	

Knowledge Mastered

Already Know	Would Like to Know
Basics of astronomy	How boys can meet girls without problems
Math, algebra, geometry	Several languages
How to read and write	Calculus
How to do research	Why some students are treated differently
Internet shortcuts	What it is about special education that seems unfair to other students
The scientific method	How to communicate with adults
What the Bill of Rights is about	Why people gossip
How to tell time	Why people steal or cheat
Why there are different time zones	How to manage time
The rules at school	How to save money
Shortcuts with homework	How to stop violence
When you lie, it just gets worse	How to take care of the Earth
How to hit free throws	All about the Bible
How to behave at church	
The rules at home	

thorough consideration. Bottom line: (1) students are real people who are living real lives right now, and (2) what students know, are interested in, and/or are good at is (a) a broad and deep foundation to connect with all learning that needs to happen now at school and (b) combined with new learning, can become the foundation for connections with all future learning.

Jason took Paula's insights and the revelations from the student surveys to go further into Extreme Teaching, to make Extreme Teaching even more extreme than he had experienced yet in his classroom and even more extreme than he had envisioned in the lesson plans he had designed. Those lesson plans were good and provided a start, but better lesson plans could be created with the addition of broader and deeper connections. The change was simple in terms of format; Jason simply added a connection preparation step in column C Tables 3.26 and 3.27 show how it works.

Table 3.26   Extreme Teaching: Lesson Plan Design for the U.S. Constitution, Part 1

With this lesson, students will make connections between what they know, what they are interested in, what they are good at and *the contents of and the meaning of the Bill of Rights (Amendments 1–10 of the U.S. Constitution).*

Column A	Column B	Column C

Step 1. What students know, are interested in and/or are good at that relates to this topic:
 	
• Rules of games.
 	
• Rules of sports.
 	
• Expressing opinions.
 	
• Going to church or deciding to not go to church.
 	
• Television and radio news programs; print newspapers; Internet news sources.
 	
• Attending events where groups of people are gathered.
	Step 2. What students need to learn and know:
	
	• The content of and the meaning of the Bill of Rights (Amendments 1–10 of the U.S. Constitution).
		Step 3. Activities that will cause this learning via connections between column A and column B, along with prior learning in this class and prior/current learning in other classes.
		
		Connection Preparation:
		
		• How to communicate with parents/guardians: show 3 ways a student could speak to a parent/guardian when asking for permission to apply for a part-time job:
		  ▪ "It's a free country. I can work if I decide to. I'm old enough."
		  ▪ "I'd like to get a part-time job so I can save up to pay for a car. I know my grades have to stay high and I still have work to do at home. I'd like to try it."
		  ▪ "My friends all work at the mall, so that's what I want to do. I'll have to quit piano lessons, but the piano was not my idea anyway."

continued

Table 3.26 (*continued*)

Column A	Column B	Column C
• Individual rights. • The destructive impact of spoken or written words that spread lies, rumors, gossip. • "He said/she said" verbal conflicts.		• Lead a discussion that explains that free speech does not suggest saying anything, anywhere at any time in any way to anyone. Freedom to speak includes the responsibility to respect freedom, rights and responsibilities of other people. <u>Teaching Activities:</u> • Have each student write a letter to the editor of the local newspaper as an exercise in freedom of speech and freedom of the press. Invite the newspaper editor to visit the class. • For parts of the Bill of Rights that relate to police action, legal procedures and court procedures, a police officer, lawyer or judge could speak to the class. The class could conduct a simulated trial. • Read the Bill of Rights aloud in class. Have students then rewrite the Bill of Rights in language more familiar to them. Does the meaning change any? • Have students evaluate school rules and school discipline procedures in terms of the Bill of Rights. • For each amendment in the Bill of Rights, identify 3 practical applications and limitations of the amendment at school, in a community and/or in a national setting. For example, the First Amendment permits peaceable assembly, but organizers of a parade need a permit from local government.

Table 3.27   Extreme Teaching: Lesson Plan Design for the U.S. Constitution, Part 2

With this lesson, students will make connections between what they know, what they are interested in, what they are good at and the *U.S. Constitution.*

Column A	Column B	Column C
Step 1. What students know, are interested in and/or are good at that relates to this topic: • The content of and the meaning of the Bill of Rights (amendments 1–10 of the U.S. Constitution). • Elections at school for class officers, student council officers or members, homecoming king and queen, club officers. • Age requirements, such as the age to get a driver's license or the age to see certain movies. • Equity issues in high school sports so that boys and girls have equal opportunity and equal support.	Step 2. What students need to learn and know: • How, when and why the U.S. Constitution has been amended to expand and/or protect the right to vote.	Step 3. Activities that will cause this learning via connections between column A and column B, along with prior learning in this class and prior/current learning in other classes. Connection Preparation: • Ask students: At a high school, should only the seniors vote for who the homecoming queen and king (both senior) will be, or should all students in the school vote? What is fair about only seniors voting? What is unfair about only seniors voting? • Should 16-year-olds be allowed to vote in the United States? They can have a job; they can pay taxes; they can drive a car—why not vote? Debate this with students. Teaching Activities: • Have students read articles, editorials and other historical materials from the time period of each change in the U.S. Constitution that impacted voting. Have students identify the reasons used by the sides in each debate over those constitutional amendments. • Have students analyze demographic data to see how various groups based on demographics—gender, age, ethnicity, income level, education level—(a) turn out to vote and (b) support different candidates. What conclusions can be reached from the analysis? • Invite the local county clerk or other election official to visit the school and conduct a voter registration drive at school. Ask the clerk or official to

continued

Table 3.27 *(continued)*

Column A	Column B	Column C
		speak to students about voting rights and voting procedures.
		• Voter participation in elections in the United States is usually low. Have students research ideas for increasing voter turnout such as voting on the weekend, voting electronically, keeping voting locations open more hours, or having all voting locations close at the same time (e.g., perhaps 10 P.M. Eastern time) in presidential election years. The students can send their ideas about increasing voter participation to their state's secretary of state.

Jason reviewed the improved lesson plan design. It seemed to work. The addition of Connection Preparation activities prior to Teaching Activities was a simple adjustment that could provide clues, previews, mental pictures, word associations and thought-starters as an introduction to the teaching activities. Then Jason saw in the Extreme Teaching idea and method a reminder of the philosophical foundation and proven results upon which Extreme Teaching is built: Socratic questioning. Paula had noticed this, too. Of course, Jason, thought to himself. How did Socrates teach? He asked sequential questions beginning with what the student knew and then, small step by small step, small question by small question, successful answer by successful answer, Socrates would lead the student from what was known to what needed to be learned.

Socrates knew the efficiency of beginning with what students know and using that knowledge to make the connection with what students need to know. He knew of the many steps that may be needed to go from what is known to what needs to be known, and he knew that sequence had meaning for the student because the student's prior knowledge and current answers became vital parts of the journey toward what needed to be learned. How did Socrates teach the Pythagorean Theorem to a student who was not skilled in geometry overall or in geometric proofs in particular? Socrates patiently, persistently and intentionally guided the student from the point of and the content of what the student knew in order to identify the necessary parts of the Pythagorean Theorem and the math steps involved. Socrates was the first Extreme Teacher! Jason was proud to modernize Socratic teaching with the Extreme Teaching process so that a noble tradition could further benefit a new generation of teachers and of students to whom Socrates may be a total stranger or a limited acquaintance.

With the inspiration that came from realizing that he was continuing and expanding the honorable tradition of Socratic teaching, Jason energetically and confidently returned to the work of creating Extreme Teaching lesson plans. He was certain that Extreme Teaching had a sufficient philosophical and theoretical foundation. He was even more certain that teachers and students cannot implement philosophy and theory in a classroom on Monday morning when first period science, math, social studies and English classes begin. Philosophy and theory can be discussed, but actions can be implemented, and Extreme Teaching is active. Extreme Teaching lesson plans are active and are ready to be implemented. It is with competent, enthusiastic and effective implementation of quality lesson plans that are designed to cause learning that students can be fascinated, can be taught and can become committed to learning at school. More lesson plans follow in tables 3.28–3.45.

Table 3.28   Extreme Teaching: Lesson Plan Design for Math Word Problems, Part 1

With this lesson, students will make connections between what they know, what they are interested in, what they are good at and *math word problems.*

Column A	Column B	Column C
Step 1. What students know, are interested in and/or are good at that relates to this topic: • Marching band. • The environment. • Assembling puzzles.	Step 2. What students need to learn and know: • How to accurately work math word problems.	Step 3. Activities that will cause this learning via connections between column A and column B, along with prior learning in this class and prior/current learning in other classes. Connection Preparation: • Along with the students, watch a 1-minute video of the local weather

continued

Table 3.28 *(continued)*

Column A	Column B	Column C

• Organizing social events.
 	
• Fashion.
 	
• Money.
 	
• Car repair.
 	
• Chess.
 	
• Shopping.
 	
• Sports.
		forecast. From that information, have each student create math word problems, such as "If the low temperature was 47 degrees and the high temperature was 67 degrees, how much did the temperature change during the day?"
		
		• Show the students a newspaper advertisement from a sporting goods store and present a word problem: If a person has $100 and buys these shoes for $71.44, 6% tax included, how much change is returned? How much more change is returned if the person uses the 20% off coupon in the advertisement?
		
		<u>Teaching Activities</u>
		
		• Create 10 word problems, each with one sentence. Examples:
		  ▪ If Mr. and Mrs. Johnson go to the movies and each pays $7.00 to get in, what's the total cost for their admission?
		  ▪ If Shawn is 16 years old today and gets a birthday present of $2.50 per year, how much will his birthday present be?
		
		Show that each problem could have been presented mathematically (e.g., 2×7 or 16×2.5), but the words created a real-life situation in which math was used. This will help students see a purpose for word problems.
		
		• Present the following problem as homework: Carla, Jennifer, Katy and Tasha are in the marching band. The band will take a trip to be in a holiday parade. They need to raise $20,000. Carla, Jennifer, Katy and Tasha organize a huge car wash at a local oil change business with this deal: Pay $5 for a car wash and get $10 off the oil change.

continued

Table 3.28 *(continued)*

Column A	Column B	Column C
		▪ If they did this on 4 Saturdays and averaged 25 cars per Saturday, how much money would they earn in the 4 Saturdays? How much is still needed for the trip? ▪ Think of 3 reasons why this event could be good business for the oil change company.

Table 3.29   Extreme Teaching: Lesson Plan Design for Math Word Problems, Part 2

With this lesson, students will make connections between what they know, what they are interested in, what they are good at and *math word problems*.

Column A	Column B	Column C
Step 1. What students know, are interested in and/or are good at that relates to this topic: • How to accurately work math word problems. • Marching band. • The environment. • Assembling puzzles. • Organizing social events. • Fashion. • Money. • Car repair. • Chess. • Shopping. • Sports.	Step 2. What students need to learn and know: • How to apply math word problem skills in everyday life.	Step 3. Activities that will cause this learning via connections between column A and column B, along with prior learning in this class and prior/current learning in other classes. Connection Preparation: Create a chart showing various costs of a gallon of gas and various rates of miles per gallon. An example is shown here:

	$1.09	$1.29	$1.49	$1.69
20 mpg	$5.45			
25 mpg		$5.16		
30 mpg			4.97	

Ask students: To drive 100 miles, what is the cost of each combination of price per gallon and miles per gallon? List 3 reasons why gas prices can change.

Teaching Activities:

• Use the school building as a resource for creating math word problems. Examples: The concession stand has $47.00 in

continued

Table 3.29 *(continued)*

Column A	*Column B*	*Column C*
		sales daily after school. 40% is profit. How much is made per week?
		• Have students create word problems based on school situations such as tickets sold at sports events, costs of textbooks, vending machine sales, amount of paper used in copy machines.
		• Have students create a word problem that relates to each class they take at school.
		• Pick any sporting event and get all of the statistics from that event. Then see how many word problems can be created. Example: Jackson High School lost a basketball game by 3 points. They hit 50% of their 20 free throws. What percentage of free throws did they need to hit to win by 1 point? To win by 2 points?
		• Use the newspaper ads from a local mall to create and to apply word problems: Example: The same jeans cost $30 at one store and $34 at another store, but sweatshirts are $19 at the first store and $16 at the second store. What's the total money you could save if you bought the lower price items at each store? Give 3 reasons why the prices might be different.

Table 3.30   Extreme Teaching: Lesson Plan Design for Percentages, Part 1

With this lesson, students will make connections between what they know, what they are interested in, what they are good at and *calculating percentages.*

Column A	Column B	Column C
Step 1. What students know, are interested in and/or are good at that relates to this topic: • Movies. • The stock market. • Concerts. • Animals. • Cooking. • Bowling. • Trucks. • Money. • Free throws and other basketball skills.	Step 2. What students need to learn and know: • How to calculate percentages.	Step 3. Activities that will cause this learning via connections between column A and column B, along with prior learning in this class and prior/current learning in other classes. Connection Preparation: Have the students consider the following scenario: There were 16,000 people attending a local concert. Of those people, 50% were aged 13–19; 25% were under age 13 and 25% were over age 19. How many people at the concert were (a) under 13, (b) 13–19, or (c) over 19. Now, list three possible entertainers who could have appealed to those 3 age groups. What else could explain the age range of the audience, besides everyone liking the music? Teaching Activities: • Put 100 pennies on a desk (Paper squares, buttons, pieces of candy or other common items can also work.) Discuss the percentages of the total when some pennies, etc. are removed. • Now, put 50 pennies (or other small objects) on the desk. Again, discuss the remaining percentages when some pennies are removed. Among the examples, be sure to include at least one identical match with the first demonstration; for example, if 40 of the 100 pennies were removed, be sure that 20 of the 50 pennies are removed so 40% is shown in two ways. Now, give each pair of students 20 paper squares. Have each pair of students separate 10% of the 20 squares, 25%, 40% and other values.

continued

Table 3.30 *(continued)*

Column A	Column B	Column C
		• Use a plastic set of bowling pins and a bowling ball. Have some or all students bowl. Ask the students: If all 10 pins are knocked down, what percentage was knocked down and what percentage are still standing? Record the results and add numbers to complete this chart:

Total pins	Pins knocked down	Percent knocked down	Pins still standing	Percent still standing
10	0	0%	10	100%
10	1	10%	9	90%
10	2	20%	8	80%
10	3	30%	7	70%
10	4	40%	6	60%
10	5	50%	5	50%
10	6	60%	4	40%
10	7	70%	3	30%
10	8	80%	2	20%
10	9	90%	1	10%
10	10	100%	0	0%

Do drill and practice on the board, on an overhead projector, and on paper so students calculate $1 \div 10$, $2 \div 10$, etc. If helpful, students can draw division problems with pictures replacing numbers: for example, $1 \div 10$ becomes a picture of 1 bowling pin over 10 bowling pins.

Table 3.31   Extreme Teaching: Lesson Plan Design for Percentages, Part 2

With this lesson, students will make connections between what they know, what they are interested in, what they are good at and *calculating percentages.*

Column A	Column B	Column C
Step 1. What students know, are interested in and/or are good at that relates to this topic: • How to calculate percentages. • Movies. • The stock market. • Concerts. • Animals. • Cooking. • Bowling. • Trucks. • Money. • Free throws and other basketball skills.	Step 2. What students need to learn and know: • What percentages mean, communicate, explain and/or reveal.	Step 3. Activities that will cause this learning via connections between column A and column B, along with prior learning in this class and prior/current learning in other classes. Connection Preparation: • Read the weather forecast from the newspaper aloud to students. If the forecast says, for example, that there is a 40% chance of rain today, see what students think this means. Tomorrow, discuss whether it rained or not. • Ask students the following question: A basketball player hits 70% of her free throws. With 1 second to go in a tied game, she has one free throw to take. What does the percentage data about this player suggest will happen? Teaching Activities: • Create an interdisciplinary unit with the physical education teacher. Have a student shoot 100 free throws while another student records the data and another student rebounds. Then have the student shoot 10 more free throws. Compare and contrast the percentage results found on the 100 and on the 10. • Create an interdisciplinary unit with the home economics/life skill teacher. Tell the students they are going to bake cookies, but they need to increase all ingredients in the cookie recipe by 50% (because, for example, 90 cookies need to be baked instead of the recipe's usual 60 cookies).

continued

Table 3.31 *(continued)*

Column A	Column B	Column C
		• Use stock market data showing a stock's current price, the high and low prices of that stock during the past year, the change in the stock's value yesterday and, using the Internet, the value of the stock right now in today's trading. Ask the students: What percentage did each stock go up/down yesterday? What percentage is each stock up/down today? What percentage is the current price of the 52-week low; of the 52-week high; what does that reveal about the stock's trend? Why is an increase of 1 point or $1 of a stock not equal in percentage to a 1-point or $1 increase of another stock?

Table 3.32   Extreme Teaching: Lesson Plan Design for Graphs, Part 1

With this lesson, students will make connections between what they know, what they are interested in, what they are good at and *graphs*.

Column A	Column B	Column C
Step 1. What students know, are interested in and/or are good at that relates to this topic: • Computers. • The stock market. • Making money. • Time management. • Television. • Careers. • Sports.	Step 2. What students need to learn and know: • How to present data using a graph.	Step 3. Activities that will cause this learning via connections between column A and column B, along with prior learning in this class and prior/current learning in other classes. Connection Preparation: • Show students a table of numbers that relate years of education to average salary. Now show the same numbers in graph form. Discuss how education can impact salary. Discuss how the table and the graph use the same data in different formats. What is the impact of each format? • Show school attendance data for teachers and for students by day of the week. Ask students: What day has the most absences? What day has the least absences? Is this random, or are there explanations?

continued

Table 3.32 *(continued)*

Column A	Column B	Column C
		Teaching Activities:

Teaching Activities:

• Using data from professional baseball teams, list the number of games each team won at home and the number of games each team won away. Present this in a table like this one:

	Won at home	Won away
Cincinnati	40	43
Los Angeles	50	33

Then have students put this information on an x/y axis graph with x = won at home and y = won away. Ask students: What additional data is of interest? Losses at home versus losses away? Number of fans at winning games versus number of fans at losing games?

• Select a basketball team. Graph the number of points scored per game against (a) the number of points scored with 3-point shots, (b) the number of points scored with 2-point shots and (c) the number of points scored from free throws.

• Using the Internet, have students view graphs of selected stocks showing the stock performance during the past 1 year, 3 years and 5 years. Ask them why the data is presented on a graph instead of as a long chart of statistics.

Table 3.33 Extreme Teaching: Lesson Plan Design for Graphs, Part 2

With this lesson, students will make connections between what they know, what they are interested in, what they are good at and *graphs.*

Column A	Column B	Column C

Step 1. What students know, are interested in and/or are good at that relates to this topic:
 	
• How to present data using a graph.
 	
• Computers.
 	
• The stock market.
 	
• Making money.
 	
• Time management.
 	
• Television.
 	
• Careers.
 	
• Sports.
 	
• Soft drinks and snacks.
	Step 2. What students need to learn and know:
	
	• How to interpret data that is presented in a graph.
		Step 3. Activities that will cause this learning via connections between column A and column B, along with prior learning in this class and prior/current learning in other classes.
		
		Connection Preparation:
		
		• Give students a graph that shows grade point averages of students (make sure no names are mentioned if actual students' information is being used) versus time spent per day by those students watching television. The graph will likely show that higher grades and fewer hours of television watching seem to go together. Have students explain this.
		
		• Show students a graph of vending machine sales at school before and after a price increase. Have them explain the results and have them suggest the best price to (a) attract customers and (b) maximize profit.
		
		Teaching Activities:
		
		• For each of the graph activities in column C of table 3.32, ask students to make conclusions about the following:
		  ▪ Is home field an advantage in baseball?
		  ▪ What type of basketball scoring seems to be most associated with more total points?
		  ▪ Based on 1-, 3- and 5-year trends and the current stock price, which stocks seem to be the best buy today for a long-term investor?
		
		• Show data to students about the cost of a personal computer during the past 20 years and the functions/

continued

Table 3.33 *(continued)*

Column A	Column B	Column C
		memory/speed/power of those computers. What conclusions are suggested by the data? What future costs and product features are suggested?

• Give students the following scenario to consider: Almost every time a store reduces the price of a 2-liter bottle of a soft drink, they sell more 2-liter bottles, as shown below.

Price	Number Sold
$1.49	30
$1.29	40
$1.09	40
$ .99	80
$ .89	100
$ .79	

- Have students make a bar graph, a line graph and one other type of graph with this information.
- What conclusions can be reached?
- What could sales be at $.79? Why?
- What other factors besides number of 2-liter bottles sold could impact the pricing decision?

Table 3.34   Extreme Teaching: Lesson Plan Design for Forms of Matter, Part 1

With this lesson, students will make connections between what they know, what they are interested in, what they are good at and *different forms of matter: liquid, solid and gas.*

Column A	Column B	Column C
Step 1. What students know, are interested in and/or are good at that relates to this topic: • Food. • Making money. • Running a marathon. • Car repair and maintenance. • Weather. • Pizza delivery. • Vocational school projects or classes. • Space exploration. • Fashion.	Step 2. What students need to learn and know: • Matter exists in different forms: liquid, solid and gas.	Step 3. Activities that will cause this learning via connections between column A and column B, along with prior learning in this class and prior/current learning in other classes. Connection Preparation: • Ask students: When someone does laundry using a washing machine and a drying machine, how are liquids, solids and gases involved? (Some answers may include solid clothes; liquid water; liquid detergent, solid detergent that dissolves into liquid; hot air to dry clothes.) • Ask students: How does liquid gasoline make a solid car move, and why is gas/exhaust released while the car is running? How do spaceship fuels function similarly or differently? Teaching Activities: • Have students compare and contrast water, ice and steam. What are some uses and purposes of each? What causes the change from water to ice or water to steam? Why does water evaporate at high temperatures but expand at low temperatures when it freezes? • Using health and exercise data, evaluate various physical activities—running, walking, yard work, riding a bicycle, sitting, swimming—in terms of calories burned and in terms of water (sweat) lost. What impact does exercise have on muscles that are solid but that have liquid (water) in/around them? • Food can be solid or liquid. Is it possible to breathe in food? Medicine can be solid (a pill) or liquid (cough syrup; an injection), but can also be a gas (mist from an

continued

Table 3.34 *(continued)*

Column A	Column B	Column C
		inhaler or direct oxygen from an oxygen tank). What reasons exist for medicines to be in one state of matter versus another state?

Table 3.35 Extreme Teaching: Lesson Plan Design for Forms of Matter, Part 2

With this lesson, students will make connections between what they know, what they are interested in, what they are good at and *different forms of matter: liquid, solid and gas.*

Column A	Column B	Column C
Step 1. What students know, are interested in and/or are good at that relates to this topic: • The fact that matter exists in different forms. • Food. • Making money. • Running a marathon. • Car repair and maintenance. • Weather. • Pizza delivery. • Vocational school projects or classes. • Space exploration. • Fashion.	Step 2. What students need to learn and know: • Business applications of various states of matter.	Step 3. Activities that will cause this learning via connections between column A and column B, along with prior learning in this class and prior/current learning in other classes. Connection Preparation: • Demonstrate different laundry detergents—liquid, powder and tablet—being poured into water. Ask students: What variations can they see in the reactions of each detergent with water? Why do companies offer consumers these options? • Discuss milk products: milk, yogurt, cheese and ice cream. Ask students: What differences and benefits are there in the various states of matter of daily products? Teaching Activities: • Display 5 liquid products, such as soft drinks, household cleaning supplies, cooking oil, honey and chocolate syrup. Have students create a solid version of each product, such as solid fabric softener sheets for liquid fabric softener. Have students name the new products, design packages for the new products, create commercials for the new products and create a

continued

Table 3.35 *(continued)*

Column A	Column B	Column C
		marketing plan for each of the new products.
		• Many products exist in a spray form such as furniture cleaner, carpet cleaner, air fresheners and insect repellant/killers. Have students do research to see if these spray products work well in a liquid or solid version of the same product. Is the science behind the function of the product or the preference of consumers the stronger factor in deciding how to design the delivery of a product? What environmental impact can spray products have?
		• Discuss with students how perfume and cologne are sold in liquid from or spray form. Ask students: Which is more popular and why? Is solid perfume possible? Why or why not? Invite a sales representative or store manager to discuss the trends in perfume/cologne that impact gifts, styles, fashion and appearance of females and males. Have students create new perfume/cologne products with names, packages, advertising and promotional marketing plans for the guest speaker to evaluate.

Table 3.36 Extreme Teaching: Lesson Plan Design for Energy, Motion and Force, Part 1

With this lesson, students will make connections between what they know, what they are interested in, what they are good at and *the scientific concepts of energy, motion and force.*

Column A	Column B	Column C
Step 1. What students know, are interested in and/or are good at that relates to this topic: • Soccer. • Skateboarding. • Cars. • Bicycles. • Music. • Football. • Playing guitar.	Step 2. What students need to learn and know: • The scientific concepts of energy, motion and force.	Step 3. Activities that will cause this learning via connections between column A and column B, along with prior learning in this class and prior/current learning in other classes. Connection Preparation: • Ask students to explain the results of this situation in terms of energy, motion and force: Two students are hurrying to class. One runs down a hallway and is about to turn left into another hall. The other is running and is about to turn right into the hall where the first student is. They get to the corner at the same time and collide. • Have each student stand up, turn around and sit down. Now, turn on a popular CD and have students do the same sequence. Ask students: How are energy, motion and force involved? What impact did hearing the music have on energy, motion and force, if any? How do energy, motion and force relate to a CD being played? Teaching Activities: • Have students define and explain the precise scientific meanings of energy, motion and force. • Have each student select a sport or job and complete a portion of this table to show how energy, motion and force are seen or used in the sport. Have everyone then complete the full chart.

continued

Table 3.36   (*continued*)

Column A	Column C		
		Energy	Motion	Force
	Baseball			
	Football			
	Basketball			
	Soccer			
	Ice skating			
	Skateboards			
	Harvesting crops			
	Assembling cars			
	Managing a fast food restaurant			
	Manufacturing bicycles			

• Take students to the gym or go to an outdoor sports field so they can measure some uses of energy, force and motion in activities such as walking, running, hitting a softball, kicking a soccer ball and jumping rope.

• Have students collect the data to compare and contrast the energy efficiency of several cars, several trucks, several sport utility vehicles and all of those versus several nonmotorized bicycles.

Table 3.37   Extreme Teaching: Lesson Plan Design for Energy, Motion and Force, Part 2

With this lesson, students will make connections between what they know, what they are interested in, what they are good at and *the scientific concepts of energy, motion and force.*

Column A	Column B	Column C
Step 1. What students know, are interested in and/or are good at that relates to this topic: • The scientific concepts of energy, motion and force. • Soccer. • Skateboarding. • Cars. • Hockey. • Music. • Riding horses. • Football. • Playing guitar.	Step 2. What students need to learn and know: • Applications of energy, motion and force in a typical home and for a typical family.	Step 3. Activities that will cause this learning via connections between column A and column B, along with prior learning in this class and prior/current learning in other classes. <u>Connection Preparation:</u> • Have students list common home appliances or machines that use energy, motion and/or force. • Have students identify how their lifestyle would change if energy (a) prices were much higher (b) supplies were limited/stopped at certain times (c) was cut off for a week due to a weather disaster. <u>Teaching Activities:</u> • Invite a guest speaker from a local utility supplier to discuss the business of providing energy. • Have a home construction company executive speak to students about new designs for energy-efficient homes. • Have students invent a home appliance of the future that is better than current appliances in terms of energy, motion and/or force. • Have students work in groups to design the home of the future, the car of the future or the computer of the future, placing emphasis on improvements in energy, motion and/or force plus realistic, desirable consumer benefits.

Table 3.38   Extreme Teaching: Lesson Plan Design for Chronological Order, Part 1

With this lesson, students will make connections between what they know, what they are interested in, what they are good at and *chronological order*.

Column A	Column B	Column C
Step 1. What students know, are interested in and/or are good at that relates to this topic:	Step 2. What students need to learn and know:	Step 3. Activities that will cause this learning via connections between column A and column B, along with prior learning in this class and prior/current learning in other classes.
• Birthdays.	• The idea of and the language of chronological order.	
• Holidays.		Connection Preparation:
• The daily school schedule.		• Have students get in a line based on the sequence of their birthdays, January 1 through December 31.
• The annual school schedule.		• Put five major historical events on the chalkboard or overhead projector for students to put in proper sequence. Use words such as century, decade, year, date and time in the discussion.
• Schedules for athletic teams.		
• Schedules for marching band competitions or other extracurricular activities.		Teaching Activities:
• How old you have to be to get a job or to get a driver's license.		• Have students work in pairs. Give each pair a set of paper rectangles with one national holiday and its date included on each piece. Have them arrange the dates in chronological order. Collect those paper pieces after each pair completes the task. Now, give each pair similar rectangles but with the name of the national holiday, but no date. Have them arrange the holidays in chronological order. Note: this also creates a teaching opportunity to be sure that students know the meaning of each national holiday.
		• Give students 10 dates from history, some B.C./B.C.E. and others A.D./C.E. Have them arrange the dates in proper chronological order. Now, tell them the 10 events/people that go with the dates and see if they can match the dates with the proper events/people. Give students math problems such as: How many years

continued

Table 3.38 *(continued)*

Column A	Column B	Column C
		were there between 1,000 B.C. and (a) 500 B.C. (b) 500 A.D. (c) now?
		• Give students a blank calendar for the next school year and have them decide when they think vacations should be, school days should be and teacher inservice days (no students) should be. Require an explanation for the recommendations. Be sure to give the state or district requirements for number of school days in a school year, etc.
		• Have students list 5 school achievements of theirs during their years in school. Have them put the 5 achievements in chronological order on paper, but have each student read his or her achievements aloud to the class in a mixed-up order. The class then has to determine the proper sequence.

Table 3.39   Extreme Teaching: Lesson Plan Design for Chronological Order, Part 2

With this lesson, students will make connections between what they know, what they are interested in, what they are good at and *chronological order.*

Column A	Column B	Column C
Step 1. What students know, are interested in and/or are good at that relates to this topic: • The idea and the language of chronological order. • Birthdays. • Holidays.	Step 2. What students need to learn and know: • Application of chronological order to personal time management.	Step 3. Activities that will cause this learning via connections between column A and column B, along with prior learning in this class and prior/current learning in other classes. <u>Connection Preparation:</u> • Borrow a practice schedule from a coach showing minute-by-minute drills and procedures for a sports practice. Have students evaluate why this is designed so precisely.

continued

Table 3.39 (*continued*)

Column A	Column B	Column C
• The daily school schedule.		• Use countdown sequences from NASA to show how time is managed during the final hours prior to a space launch.
• The annual school schedule.		
• Schedules for athletic teams.		Teaching Activities:
• Schedules for marching band competitions or other extracurricular activities.		• Show a video of the final 1 minute of a very close basketball game when both teams use time outs, make substitutions, foul on purpose and otherwise try to control the clock. Have students explain the reasons for each time management action.
• How old you have to be to get a job; to get a driver's license.		• Have students keep a log for 1 week to record how they actually used their time. Then review with students the major categories of time usage: school, sleep, study, family activities, job, friends, extracurricular activities, church, meetings, TV, other entertainment, meals and others. Have students identify areas in which time was wasted. Students can now create their improved schedule for the upcoming week.
• Space launch countdowns.		
		• Have each student interview adults and older students to get time management ideas. Have each student report to the class the best idea he or she heard.
		• Invite a person who must manage time so each second counts (e.g., hospital emergency room personnel) to speak to the class about time management skills.

Table 3.40   Extreme Teaching: Lesson Plan Design for How to Compare and Contrast, Part 1

With this lesson, students will make connections between what they know, what they are interested in, what they are good at and *how to compare and contrast.*

Column A	Column B	Column C
Step 1. What students know, are interested in and/or are good at that relates to this topic:	Step 2. What students need to learn and know:	Step 3. Activities that will cause this learning via connections between column A and column B, along with prior learning in this class and prior/current learning in other classes.
• Reading books.	• The idea of comparing and contrasting.	**Connection Preparation:**
• The Internet.		• Have students list everything that is similar about elementary school and middle school to see how they compare. Then have students list everything that is different between elementary school and middle school.
• Business.		
• Space travel.		
• Cars.		
• Sports.		• Have students create categories for the compare and contrast lists of elementary and middle schools: for example, numbers (elementary school had fewer students) or schedule (elementary school had recess).
• Acting.		
• Singing.		
• Animals.		
• Fishing.		
• Trivia.		**Teaching Activities:**
• Dances.		• Give students a chart with different age groups and different events/ experiences such as the one below:
• Birthdays.		
• Good grades.		

	Six-year-olds	Sixteen-year-olds	Teachers	Parents/ guardians
Their own birthday				
School dances				
Snow				
Popular music				
Homework				
The Internet				
Curfew				
School dress code				
Grades				

continued

Table 3.40 *(continued)*

Column A	Column B	Column C
		Have students will identify their perceived opinion of each age group toward each event/experience. What comparisons are seen? What contrasts are seen?
		• Conduct 3 different experiments in science class. Ask students: What comparisons can be made in the hypothesis, procedure and findings? What contrasts?
		• Select 5 major events in U.S. history that the students know well. Ask students: What comparisons can be made in the causes of, impact of and lessons learned from these events? What contrasts?
		• Select several sports or games. Have students compare and contrast rules, skills, demands, fan interest, demographic appeal and equipment/costs involved with each.
		• Have students read a print advertisement for a product, listen to a radio advertisement for the same product and watch a television advertisement for the same product. Then, have the students compare/contrast the advertisements for content, appeal, creativity, impact and other factors you and students can identify.

Table 3.41 Extreme Teaching: Lesson Plan Design for How to Compare and Contrast, Part 2

With this lesson, students will make connections between what they know, what they are interested in, what they are good at and *how to compare and contrast*.

Column A	Column B	Column C
Step 1. What students know, are interested in and/or are good at that relates to this topic: • The idea of comparing and contrasting.	Step 2. What students need to learn and know: • Application of compare and contrast.	Step 3. Activities that will cause this learning via connections between column A and column B, along with prior learning in this class and prior/current learning in other classes. Connection Preparation: • Play a song that is popular now. Then play a popular song from 20

continued

Table 3.41 *(continued)*

Column A	Column B	Column C
• Reading. • The Internet. • Business. • Space travel. • Cars. • Sports. • Acting. • Singing. • Animals. • Fishing. • Trivia. • Dances. • Birthdays. • Good grades.		years ago. Ask the students: What is similar and what is different? How do entertainers know what people will like? • Show a school yearbook picture of fashions from last year and from 20 years ago. Ask the students: What is similar? What is different? Have them predict the next fashion fad. Teaching Activities: • Present information about many different jobs—skills needed, training required, education required, average wages, opportunities for future career advancement. Have students compare and contrast the jobs. Now, have students select jobs of interest to them and research the necessary preparation to qualify for the jobs. Have students take interest/career aptitude tests to see how their stated interest compares/contrasts with their measured aptitudes. • Have students use websites, catalogues, interviews with alumni and independent rankings to compare/contrast colleges, universities and technical/vocational schools that are of serious interest to the students as schools they may attend after high school. Have students use websites, official publications, interviews with veterans and information from recruiters to compare/contrast work/career opportunities with the U.S. military. • Have students select 5 common consumer product categories such as laundry detergent, hair shampoo, peanut butter, soft drinks and bread. Have students select 5 different brands in each product category to compare/contrast factors such as prices at different stores, packaging, ingredients, label information and marketing. Have students create a rating scale to evaluate the products.

Table 3.42   Extreme Teaching: Lesson Plan Design for Accepting Responsibility, Part 1

With this lesson, students will make connections between what they know, what they are interested in, what they are good at and *accepting responsibility.*

Column A	Column B	Column C
Step 1. What students know, are interested in and/or are good at that relates to this topic: • Baby-sitting. • Training animals. • Volunteer work at church or a hospital. • The juvenile justice system. • Car and road laws. • Business. • Getting a job. • The Internet. • Making good grades. • Staying out of trouble. • Church youth group activities. • Clubs at school.	Step 2. What students need to learn and know: • The meaning and the importance of accepting responsibility.	Step 3. Activities that will cause this learning via connections between column A and column B, along with prior learning in this class and prior/current learning in other classes. Connection Preparation: Discuss these case studies: • A 13-year-old is told by his or her parent/guardian to have all homework finished by 6:00 because the family is going to a 6:30 dinner and program at church tonight. The homework is not finished by 6:00. What happens next? What could prevent this problem? • As a teacher collects books at the end of the school year a student says, "I don't have my book. I think somebody stole it." What could the student have done to avoid this problem at this late date in the school year? Teaching Activities: • Have students interview family members about the importance of accepting responsibility and report their findings to the class. • Have students read biographies of responsible people and identify what responsibilities were accepted, why those responsibilities were accepted and what difference being responsible made. Have students consider the different results if the same people in the biographies had been irresponsible.

continued

Table 3.42 *(continued)*

Column A	Column B	Column C
		• Invite a speaker—business owner, firefighter, college coach, police officer, lawyer, judge—to discuss the importance of and the meaning of responsibility.
		• Have students create typical school scenarios to show the responsible way to handle situations at school.
		• Have students present ideas from the American legal system about responsibility. Conduct a mock trial to see how laws, lawyers, juries and judges assign responsibility.
		• Have students write a definition of responsibility and an application of that to their various roles as family member, student, club member, friend, athlete, church member and others as they apply. Ask students: What aspects of responsibility are similar in each role? What aspects vary in importance with one role versus another? Why?

Table 3.43 Extreme Teaching: Lesson Plan Design for Accepting Responsibility, Part 2

With this lesson, students will make connections between what they know, what they are interested in, what they are good at and *accepting responsibility.*

Column A	Column B	Column C
Step 1. What students know, are interested in and/or are good at that relates to this topic: • The meaning of and the importance of accepting responsibility. • Baby-sitting. • Training animals. • Volunteer work at church or a hospital. • The juvenile justice system. • Car and road laws. • Business. • Getting a job • The Internet. • Making good grades. • Staying out of trouble. • Church youth group activities. • Clubs at school.	Step 2. What students need to learn and know: • How to accept responsibility.	Step 3. Activities that will cause this learning via connections between column A and column B, along with prior learning in this class and prior/current learning in other classes. Connection Preparation: • Give students a real job application from a local business or employment agency. Have each student complete an application. Discuss how accepting responsibility is part of what an employer looks for in an employee. • Discuss this statement with students: If you have the ability to make an A grade, you have the responsibility to yourself to make the A grade. Teaching Activities: • Have the class select a school service project, such as a paper recycling program. From start to finish, have the students create the entire recommendation and implementation plan. The students can then manage the school service project, frequently evaluating what is working well and what needs to improve. • Select 5 to 10 current news stories with a wide range of topics from politics to business, from sports to courtroom, from entertainment to international events. Ask the students: In what ways are people in those stories properly accepting responsibility? In what ways are people in those stories being

continued

Table 3.43 *(continued)*

Column A	Column B	Column C
		irresponsible? Create with the students a report card for responsibility to help students learn how to observe, measure and identify evidence of responsibility.
		• Have students research the lives of accomplished people, famous or not, with emphasis on what influenced, guided, inspired and motivated each person to accept the responsibility of being very productive. Students could use many sources: reading biographies, conducting interviews, watching documentaries and others.

Table 3.44 Extreme Teaching: Lesson Plan Design for the Scientific Method, Part 1

With this lesson, students will make connections between what they know, what they are interested in, what they are good at and *the idea of the scientific method.*

Column A	Column B	Column C
Step 1. What students know, are interested in and/or are good at that relates to this topic: • Concerts. • Dating. • Musical instruments. • Cooking. • Autograph collecting. • Yard work, gardening. • How to graduate from high school early. • Shortcuts with homework.	Step 2. What students need to learn and know: • The idea of the scientific method.	Step 3. Activities that will cause this learning via connections between column A and column B, along with prior learning in this class and prior/current learning in other classes. Connection Preparation: • Discuss the following topic as a class: Will famous people respond to a written request for an autograph? Find examples from books that tell of attempts to request autographs from celebrities by letter. Show what parts of the attempts followed the scientific method and which did not. • Ask the students: When a concert promoter makes plans for a concert, what steps must be followed? How are these steps "scientific"?

continued

Table 3.44 *(continued)*

Column A	Column B	Column C
• Getting accepted to a good college.		Teaching Activities:
		• By direct instruction, teach the scientific method. Be sure that key vocabulary is mastered: *question, hypothesis, dependent variable, independent variable, procedure, data, analyze* and *conclusion.*
		• Using the scientific method, have students design research for this question: could our school make money if a fast food restaurant were given a contract to sell food here before school starts in the morning, at lunch, after school and at extracurricular events?
		• Discuss the following with students: A sports team is losing most of its games. The coach changes the practice activities to give the athletes much more repetition of basic skills until every team member masters those skills. What results in future games could be expected? Give 3 reasons to explain each of these possible outcomes: (a) the team continues to lose, (b) the team begins to win or (c) the team wins some games and loses others.
		• Discuss what can go wrong with an experiment that is conducted using the scientific method. What limits are on the scientific method? The scientific method is imperfect; have students explain why.
		• Ask the students: When a person tries a new recipe provided by a friend to cook something, is the person using the scientific method? Did the person who created the new recipe follow the scientific method? What similarities and differences are there in the scientific method when (a) creating a new recipe or (b) following a new recipe?

Table 3.45 Extreme Teaching: Lesson Plan Design for the Scientific Method, Part 2

With this lesson, students will make connections between what they know, what they are interested in, what they are good at and the scientific method.

Column A	Column B	Column C

Step 1. What students know, are interested in and/or are good at that relates to this topic:
 	
• The idea of the scientific method.
 	
• Concerts.
 	
• Dating.
 	
• Musical instruments.
 	
• Cooking.
 	
• Autograph collecting.
 	
• Yard work, gardening.
 	
• How to graduate from high school early.
 	
• Shortcuts with homework.
 	
• Getting accepted to a good college.
	Step 2. What students need to learn and know:
	
	• Application of and experience using the scientific method.
		Step 3. Activities that will cause this learning via connections between column A and column B, along with prior learning in this class and prior/current learning in other classes.
		
		<u>Connection Preparation:</u>
		
		• Invite several college freshmen and a school counselor to speak to the class to answer questions about:
		  ■ The process of applying to and selecting a college.
		  ■ Ways to move through high school faster:
		    o Internet courses
		    o Summer school
		    o Independent study
		  ■ Study skills that are efficient and productive.
		
		• Discuss the information from the college students and the school counselor in terms of the scientific method.
		
		<u>Teaching Activities:</u>
		
		• Have every student design and complete a science fair project that is in full compliance with the scientific method.
		
		• Have students evaluate a week of their life in terms of the scientific process: they should analyze what happens when they make decisions about whom to date, about how to use time, about money, about how to behave, about what to say or not to say. Are those decisions based on any scientific method thinking or not? How could the scientific method apply in typical moment-to-moment, day-to-day matters?
		
		• Discuss the following scenario: Imagine that your school building is

continued

Table 3.45   (continued)

Column A	Column B	Column C
		going to be renovated in 3 years or that your school district will build a new school in 3 years. Using the scientific method, design the renovated or new school.

Note to the reader: We will return to Jason Prather in a moment, but for now it is your turn to write. Please review the lesson plans in tables 3.1 to 3.24. In many of the plans, you will see a * toward the top of the right column. This is where you are to insert your ideas for Connection Preparation activities that could be logically and effectively added to each of those lessons. When you finish with that, please use the two lesson plans that follow in tables 3.46 and 3.47 (if this is not your book, please use a separate sheet of paper) to create an Extreme Teaching plan on a topic that you could use with your current or future students, colleagues or constituents.

"Now what?" Jason asked himself. "I know Extreme Teaching works because I see my students respond to it every day. Socrates was right."

Table 3.46   Extreme Teaching: Lesson Plan Design for (a)_____, Part 1

With this lesson, students will make connections between what they know, what they are interested in, what they are good at and (a) _____.

Column A	Column B	Column C
Step 1. What students know, are interested in and/or are good at that relates to this topic:	Step 2. What students need to learn and know:	Step 3. Activities that will cause this learning via connections between column A and column B, along with prior learning in this class and prior/current learning in other classes. Connection Preparation: Teaching Activities:

Table 3.47   Extreme Teaching: Lesson Plan Design for (a) _____, Part 2

With this lesson, students will make connections between what they know, what they are interested in, what they are good at and (a) _____.

Column A	Column B	Column C
Step 1. What students know, are interested in and/or are good at that relates to this topic: • Subject from Part 1 of this lesson.	Step 2. What students need to learn and know:	Step 3. Activities that will cause this learning via connections between column A and column B, along with prior learning in this class and prior/current learning in other classes. Connection Preparation: Teaching Activities:

Reminder: An Extreme Teaching lesson does not stand alone as a finite learning experience; rather, each lesson leads to other lessons or connects with other lessons. The format above is designed so that one lesson is not created by itself but connects with at least one other lesson. For example, the lesson about adding fractions (table 3.1) flowed easily into and connected easily with the next lesson about subtracting fractions (table 3.2); however, these lessons could be used at separate times as well as in a sequential pair.

When teachers begin with what students already know and then lead those students step by step through sequential, logical, sensible and feasible questions or other learning activities, the students can master any information, knowledge or skill. This is a different way of looking at students and at teaching than most people are used to. Contrary to what we tend to assume, students do not come to schools and classrooms without some prior learning, experience or awareness. Maybe Extreme Teaching is not fancy enough or expensive enough to be taken seriously, but it is what it is. It is taking what students know, are good at, are interested in and using that foundation to make connections with what needs to be learned in class. It helps make school real. It helps make school matter. It helps inspire students to make a commitment to school. It helps give teachers some rewarding career experiences. Everyone wins. "But," Jason thought, "How do I get the bureaucracy of committees, task forces, boards, policies, regulations and laws to see that Socrates was right and that teaching is a very direct human adventure in interactive, adventurous learning?"

Jason knew what to do. Call Paula Hammisch. "Paula, I've made the revisions you requested. Extreme Teaching is ready to be presented to our think group. What should we do next?"

"Jason, I'm so glad you called today. The superintendent is enraged. The school board members are furious. Everyone is screaming about test scores. The newspaper keeps running stories about test scores. We don't have time for you and me to meet first and then for you to make changes in your recommendations and then for the think group to meet; we need a solution now. How soon can our think group meet? I hope it's right now."

Jason spoke cautiously, "Extreme Teaching isn't going to create great newspaper stories instantly. It may not relieve today's frustration of the superintendent and the school board. It reminds us of what works and shows us how to implement a solid idea and a solid teaching method. Sure, I can meet with our committee soon, but I think it's best to give them a copy of the Extreme Teaching proposal I've written, give them time to read it and then meet. That's more productive than having a meeting in which participants did no advance thinking or reading to prepare. So, I'll bring you a copy today, I'll take a copy to the rest of the group today and we can meet in two or three days. Can you please check with everyone once to schedule the meeting and then again to confirm our meeting date, time, place and agenda?"

"Sure, Jason. Consider it done. I hope your Extreme Teaching idea is at least part of what we need to get these test scores up. Thanks for the extra work that you're doing."

Jason began to reflect. How, he wondered, does the purity, the joy, the frustration, the power, the humanity, the difficulty of teaching get communicated to a bureaucracy or to the media? Bureaucracies understand laws, regulations, policies, budgets, meetings, politics and taxes. The media thrive on seeking the next Watergate or other sensational scandal. Teaching understands the vibrant, caring, dynamic, fascinating interaction among ideas, students and teachers that causes learning. Perhaps the think group committee—a committee by any other name is still a committee—could answer Jason's question.

Paula Hammisch: Everyone is busy with school, meetings and families, so let's get started now. I want to thank Jason for putting together his ideas about Extreme Teaching. He brought each of us a summary of the

Extreme Teaching idea, concept and method. He has given us lots of lesson plans on a big variety of topics. If you've read Jason's material you can see the type of classroom experiences Extreme Teaching can provide for students and teachers. Jason, let's start with you. First, let's all remember, our group is charged with making a recommendation that the superintendent can take to the school board for an action plan that will increase test scores throughout our school district. I know tests and test scores are controversial, but those tests are required by the state, and the test scores are how the state measures each school. Like it or not, no matter what else we do for students, test scores must go up or the state will consider us as failing. That is reality. Jason, lead the way, please.

Jason Prather: Thanks, Paula. I've been a teacher for 38 of my 37 years of life. By that I mean that teaching chose me before I was born. I'm a teacher 100 percent. Teaching is more than what I do; it is who I am. So, when I think of how education needs to improve, my thoughts turn to how the effectiveness of teaching can improve. I know that most teachers put in lots of hours, put in evenings and weekends to grade papers, spend personal money for classroom materials. I also know that more and more students just give up on schoolwork. They may do enough to pass. They may make good grades to avoid family criticism. Some may actually like school, but more and more students seem to make less and less commitment to schoolwork.

   Why? I've conducted research with thousands of students in our community and from other cities or states. I attend conferences, workshops or other events for students. I talk to students at these events and they say with one very clear, passionate and convincing voice: "School is boring." When I ask for details they add, "School is out of touch with me and my life." I know the adults are in charge. I know schoolwork is work; it is not and cannot be intended to be play or fun. Schoolwork can be fascinating, and when people work on something that fascinates them it can feel like play and it can seem like fun. How do teachers fascinate students? I'd suggest that we begin with what students already know, already are good at and/or already are interested in and connect those ideas, experiences, knowledge and talents that students bring with them with what we need them to learn. For example, if a school rule requires students to follow a dress code and the students hate the dress code, a teacher has a perfect connection between how school rules are made and enforced and how cities, states, nations and ancient civilizations made and enforced rules or laws. Reading chapter 6 in the World Civilization book and answering questions about that can be superficial, ordinary, pointless and boring, but if that chapter helps a student learn how to impact the school dress code rule, well, chapter 6 could become fascinating because it matters, it connects with real life right now and right here. That's the idea.

Test scores are low or are not increasing enough for many reasons. We can't control all those reasons. But we, as educators, can control what happens at school. When we fascinate students in classrooms, we gain their commitment to school. When we connect school learning with the real lives students are living now, we show students that we take them seriously as real people. Students who are fascinated by school and who are taken seriously by school are more likely to commit to school, are more likely to learn at school and then, you know what? Those students will do better on tests. The increased test scores will happen not because we became obsessed with tests but because we became magnificently obsessed with fascinating students through teaching and learning experiences that connect their existing interests, talents and knowledge to new knowledge. Then, they can become lifelong learners in addition to succeeding at school now.

Extreme Teaching goes to the extreme of what students already know, are interested in and/or are good at and builds upon that with new, meaningful learning now, learning that is extremely fascinating. This new learning becomes a solid foundation for the known and unknown adventures, duties and challenges students will face in the future.

You've read the Extreme Teaching material. You know the results from my classroom—that's been documented in reports, e-mails, charts and presentations. The results show that students learn, pass, excel, commit, get fascinated and seem to stay fascinated. Let's see what everyone else is thinking.

Angela Overstreet: Well, Katie and Ken and I have already discussed this idea with Jason. Before Katie speaks for us, I'll say that some students are interested in or are good at or already know a lot about drugs, stealing, getting drunk and getting pregnant. Are we going to use those topics, since some students are interested in those?

Jason Prather: We already do use those topics. We teach against abuse of alcohol and other drugs. We teach sober, safe driving. We punish any stealing at school. We follow the approved curriculum about responsible, proper, legal, moral behavior in dating relationships. If a student has an improper interest, we can ignore that or we can seek to correct that.

Katie Fletcher: Here's the point. Our school district is crazy over test scores. There are very clear and certain test-taking methods that will get scores up. If our students knew how to take these tests, which for good or bad are different from most day-to-day school tests, they would show a big improvement. All we have to do for the next round of tests in order to show a big increase in scores is to work with students to practice, practice, practice on how to take the tests. We could give tests like these throughout the year in our classes. The scores will go up and the critical newspaper stories will stop.

Paula Hammisch: OK. Test-taking skill helps, but students will show limited improvement that way. Once the benefit of the test-taking skill ends, the only improvement comes from students knowing more than they ever knew about every subject we teach. We can't just practice test-taking skills and declare victory. Students must learn more and must learn better about everything.

Ken Belton: Angela, Katie and I did talk about Extreme Teaching. We are willing to try it. It sounds pretty neat, actually. We just think that some teachers will resent having to change what they do. We also think, well, the superintendent always brings in people to train us in new ideas. The school board seems to always want people from business and industry to come train us in their methods of getting the most out of people. Can the superintendent and the school board be satisfied with something as simple as a different way of teaching, or do they need to see lots of expensive, politically correct experts come tell us what to do for our students?

Paula Hammisch: It's my job to deal with the politics of the superintendent and the school board. This group needs to make a recommendation now, so I can take that recommendation to the superintendent, and then I'll help the superintendent make the recommendation to the school board.

Jason Prather: We could meet longer, but there's no need. I suggest we recommend that all teachers in our district be trained in Extreme Teaching. I also suggest we recommend that each teacher format some tests to use throughout the year to match the format of the state's annual tests. This will help the students learn content in general while helping students improve in test-taking skills.

Paula Hammisch: If everyone agrees, that's what I'll take to the superintendent. OK? Fine. Thanks for your time, work and help.

While driving home, Jason reflected further about students, school, test scores and Extreme Teaching. He also thought of soccer, because his son had practice today and his daughter had a game. Why did his children and everyone on their teams work so hard at soccer, he wondered? Because it was real right now. School needs to be real right now for students just as soccer is real right now for Jason's children. The same age group that hates school loves other parts of life. As he'd reflected so many times before, school could fascinate students. Extreme Teaching could help fascinate students, who will then learn and who will take that learning with them as they encounter the next round of tests. If you fascinate them, they will learn. If they learn, their test scores will improve. Socrates really was right.

CHAPTER 4

A Classroom Visit

Socrates was right. Socrates is still right. Begin with what the student knows. Ask precise sequential questions to lead the student from the known to the unknown, from the already learned to the next to be learned, from the current skill to new skills and from the current interest to a new, deeper, broader application or development of that interest and of related interests.

Extreme Teaching broadens the Socratic method. Extreme Teaching seeks connections between (a) the variety of existing interests, existing skills and existing knowledge of students and (b) a variety of new interests, new skills and new knowledge for students. When Plato presented Socratic questioning in the essay "Meno," he showed math knowledge leading to more math knowledge via Socratic questioning. Extreme Teaching, however, seeks even wider and deeper connections. A teacher could use a student's knowledge of music to lead to new knowledge in math. A student's skill in gardening could lead to new understanding of the scientific method. These extreme connections seek to show students an often-unrealized value to learning at school and seek to inspire new commitment from students to the work required for learning at school to happen.

It is the essay entitled "Meno," (part of *The Dialogues of Plato*) that provides clear insight into the Socratic philosophy of learning. "Meno" also addresses other topics such as, What is virtue? What is a virtue? Is virtue learned? and Is virtue acquired by or inherent in the human? "Meno" also includes some of Jason Prather's favorite thoughts about education. Jason often reflects upon this statement by Socrates: "All learning is but recollection."

What Jason refers to as what students know, are interested in and/or are good at is similar to what Socrates refers to as recollection. That which students know, are interested in and/or are good at is a vast foundation for further knowledge, new interests and new skills. As Socrates would guide a student through precise sequential questions to take what he or she knows and to extend that knowledge one bit of information at a time, Jason Prather would take what is known by, of interest to or is a talent/skill of a student and extend or connect that to the next bit of information, the next idea, the next skill to be learned at school.

Socrates makes another statement in "Meno" that has perplexed, amazed, invigorated, intrigued and inspired Jason Prather with each reading of, analysis of, contemplation of or reflection on the statement: "And if the truth of all things always existed in the soul, then the soul is immortal. Wherefore be of good cheer, and try to recollect what you do not know, or rather what you do not remember." Jason has not used that Platonic perspective as a theological premise, although it could serve that purpose; rather, Jason has reflected upon and acted upon the challenge to cause learning by showing students how much they already know, by showing them how much more they can learn by connecting what they already know with what is yet to be learned and by creating activities in which students just plain have to think more and better than they would otherwise.

Jason knows that all students can learn, because every student who comes to school has already learned something and may have learned much. Accepting as real, valid and useful what students already know, are interested in and/or are good at is the starting point for connections, ideas, activities and learning in Jason Prather's Extreme Teaching classroom. Jason is bold enough to think that improvements in education could come from an idea as old as Socrates, but also from other sources as new as the talents, skills, interests, ideas and knowledge of today's students.

Socrates was right, but did Socrates live in a simpler time when bureaucracy and political correctness were less powerful than now? His trial perhaps suggests that bureaucracy and political correctness may have been long-standing challenges to progress and to truth.

After meeting with Jason and the rest of the think group and formulating a recommendation for the superintendent about how to raise test scores, Paula Hammisch worked with the superintendent and the school board in an open discussion at a school board meeting. The discussion became a debate. The debate became a dispute. The dispute became a diversion. The diversion almost became a disaster. Finally, Paula offered a politically correct, bureaucratically acceptable compromise that had three steps.

First, all teachers, administrators and central office personnel would attend a two-day training program entitled Demographic Education, Academic Results (DEAR). One person in the audience suggested that the name of the training should be Demographic Education, Academic Theory with the acronym DEATH, because the training would likely bore everyone to death and because the training would likely go the way of so many other past trends or fads in education—forgotten, criticized, resented, dead.

The Demographic Education, Academic Results training states that teachers must teach differently for each demographic group in order for students to learn best. This would mean teaching differently for white females, white males, black females, black males, Hispanic females, Hispanic males, Asian females, Asian males, Native American females, Native American males, all other females by unique demographic group and all other males by unique demographic group. Nonsense. Why is it nonsense? Because in an area of education in which test score results are never a problem—extracurricular activities— coaches and sponsors do not vary instruction for each demographic group. Do football coaches teach blocking and tackling differently to one demographic group than another? Does the marching band instructor vary the marching band practice, routine, show or schedule by demographic group? No.

Demographic Education, Academic Results training would cost the school district $14,000 for the expert trainer who would come in, talk for six hours for each of the two days, take the money and leave. The newspaper would print positive stories. The press conference would be impressive. Interest groups would applaud. Most educators attending the conference would eagerly anticipate breaks, lunch and the end of the second day. They would forget what they heard as they drove home from the training sessions, but the two days of training sessions would be very visible to the public and to local opinion leaders.

Second, the school district created two new central office positions: Total Education Support and Technology (TEST) coordinators. One TEST coordinator would work with administrators, faculty and staff at elementary schools, the other with administrators, faculty and staff at secondary schools. In reality, the TEST coordinators were told to provide the necessary overall support and the necessary specific technology guidance to help schools get test scores up quickly.

Third, Jason Prather's school would implement Extreme Teaching. Some of the teachers at that school had already borrowed Jason's methods. Some of the teachers had created interdisciplinary projects with Jason. Jason had already provided training in his teaching method at a faculty meeting. The response to the training was favorable, and the teachers seemed open to further training from Jason—who insisted on providing that training at no charge. Jason's extra pay would be when students and teachers benefited from Extreme Teaching. He really saw no reason for his employer to pay him extra to share ideas with colleagues. He hoped to be given suggestions from other teachers during discussions at his training sessions, because trading successful ideas is symbiotic.

So, the school district began a three-part endeavor to increase test scores. Jason knew what he needed to do first. He would write a verbatim script of a typical Extreme Teaching lesson from his classroom. Jason wanted his colleagues in the training session to get a genuine understanding of what is said and done when Extreme Teaching happens. No video camera would be used, because students might be tempted to "perform" for the camera. Only a small audiotape recorder would be used. The script of the class is shown here.

EXTREME TEACHING: JASON PRATHER

Lesson Topic: How to Present Data Using a Graph

"Good morning. Welcome to the Tuesday episode of fascinating indoor thinking. Please begin working on or continue working on the thought-starter activity, which, of course, is on the board in the upper right corner as always. You'll need two or three minutes to complete that. I'll do high technology attendance checking on the computer, and then we'll trade ideas."

Mr. Prather needed only a few seconds to complete the computer checks that recorded attendance for the class. He then picked up a clipboard that had one sheet of paper attached to it. That paper had each student's name on a grid to keep track of class participation each day. Mr. Prather had years of evidence to confirm that as students participate in class more, they learn more. So, he kept notes about and assigned points for class participation, which helped show the students that he took their questions, their answers, their thoughts, their involvement, their attention and their interaction seriously. Mr. Prather put the class participation results on paper throughout each class because he believed that what gets written down gets measured and what gets measured gets done.

As Mr. Prather walked up and down the rows of students, he was pleased to see everyone working on the thought-starter topic. Sure, that was no more than what they were expected to do, but when students did what they were supposed to do, Mr. Prather got the opportunity to acknowledge that. Another belief of Jason Prather's was that, in education, teachers get more of what they reward. When students worked, learned, obeyed and cooperated, they deserved more than not being punished, Mr. Prather thought. Usually in classrooms, when students were bad they got punished, and when students were good they got the absence of punishment as their reward. But that equation was imbalanced. From points to praise, from candy to prizes, Mr. Prather's students knew they were in an arena of classroom capitalism: If you worked, if you produced, if you learned, you got paid.

Today's thought starter was "draw a picture of a scoreboard. It could be from any athletic event. Include applicable numbers such as the score, time remaining, quarter or half or inning or period, time outs left and other useful data that could or should appear on scoreboards. Your scoreboard design can be creative so it looks different and better than existing scoreboards."

The topic for the day was how to present data using a graph. Mr. Prather was not limiting the graph use to one academic subject. Graphs could be used in math, science, social studies, language arts, computer class, art, physical education, music, international language, journalism, vocational studies and all other classes. Mr. Prather thought that beginning with the scoreboard thought starter should give each student some initial success in class, should involve each student with the idea of presenting data, and should connect graph use with students' prior knowledge or interest or skill—they have seen scoreboards and may have been impacted directly by the results shown on a scoreboard. As Jason noticed that every student had completed the thought starter, he marked on his class participation chart five points for everyone. Students were aware of this measurement, but they worked well primarily because Mr. Prather created assignments, lessons and activities that were interesting, worthwhile, imaginative and fascinating. Plus, the work in class was real—it connected to the lives of the students, who, Mr. Prather believed, were real people living real lives right now.

"Thomas, what conclusions could be reached by looking at the numbers you put on the scoreboard?"

"Well, you could see that the game went into extra innings. It is still tied after 12 innings. You could tell how many hits and errors there were. I included special prices from the concession stand. Each inning, something is sold at a lower price than usual. There is the time of day. I included a super big screen to show instant replays."

"Great, Thomas. That tells us a lot. We could almost write a newspaper story about the game from the statistics you gave us. Who's next? OK, Angel."

"I decided to put a scoreboard in the store where I work. It's a fast food place, so the numbers show how many people have been in so far, what the special deals are, how much we've sold today of the most popular items. I even included an unadvertised special area on the scoreboard. If we need to hurry up and sell a lot of something, we can put a lower price up on the scoreboard until we sell out of that."

Mr. Prather was delighted. "Wow, Angel. Neat idea. A scoreboard at a fast food restaurant. You may have just invented the menu of the future."

Tasha's hand was up, so Mr. Prather called on her. "Hey, this scoreboard idea could work at school. The one I drew was from a gym and shows basketball numbers like we've all seen, but why not have a scoreboard in the main hall or in the cafeteria? We could put message board-type announcements on it. Scores of recent games. Cafeteria menu. Events coming up. Number of people here today. Number of days until summer vacation."

Jeremy joined in. "My scoreboard is from a football stadium, but maybe it could be portable. Those smart boards we use with computers in some classes move from room to room. Maybe a scoreboard could go from outside to inside."

Big ideas were being thought up. Mr. Prather was encouraged. "Marian, tell us about your drawing."

She paused and then asked, "Could I just draw it up on the board, please?"

"Of course."

The whole class knew of Marian's art talent. Everyone watched with genuine appreciation for Marian's skill as she turned a blank white marker board into a three-dimensional, multicolored, multifunction, state-of-the-art scoreboard. There were two big TV screens, one for continuous live action and one for instant replays. There were statistics about the game being played: free throws, two-point shots, three-point shots, fouls, time outs, turnovers, rebounds. There were moving message board advertisements from sponsors who had paid for the board. The class applauded as Marian finished. Her skill in art was matched by her skill in basketball, and Mr. Prather loved seeing both talents put to such great academic use.

"Great job, Marian. Let's use some of the data from your scoreboard to move into how to present data in graph form. We'll start with some easy options and then get more sophisticated. Also, we'll just draw graphs by hand now, but in a day or two we'll put all the data into the computer, and you guys can create endless graphs with colors, shapes, designs and features that will reinvent the concept of animation. OK, in Marian's example of a scoreboard, the score of the game is 56–53 with eight seconds left to play. Let's imagine what happens in those final eight seconds."

Mr. Prather could have skipped this discussion. The final eight seconds of the game were not vital to making graphs, but this was a one- or two-minute discussion that could inspire imagination, creativity, thinking and interest. The resulting work on graphs would probably be more meaningful and more interesting.

"I know, I know!"

"OK. Brittany tell us." When students were sincerely eager to talk about the current topic, Mr. Prather could live with a spoken word rather than a raised hand.

"Well, the team with 56 points just scored with two free throws because the other team had to foul to get the ball back. The team with 53 points has an eight-second drill to get a fast three-point shot. It works, and with two seconds left they hit a three-point shot to tie the game. The other team calls time out and they set up a play. When time is back in, that team throws the ball in, but it gets intercepted, I guess you call it. As the buzzer sounds, a shot is in the air. Everyone watches as the ball goes toward the goal. Will the team that just tied it up 56–56 now hit the last-second shot and win 58–56? Yes! The shot goes in."

The class cheered; Brittany's talent in speech and drama was obvious. She had an internship with a local radio station and covered high school sports for the station.

"Great story, Brittany. That's an exciting finish. There is a lot that can happen in the final eight seconds of a basketball game. We should use that topic for a thought starter soon. OK, scholars, let's create a graph. We'll use that score of 58–56 to get started, but first, what's the idea of a graph? Why not just say the score was 58–56 and that's that?"

Shawn knew. "Pictures, Mr. Prather. Graphs are about pictures. We learned that in home economics class when we had to change recipes to feed twice the number of people as the recipe was written for. With all the fractions in the recipe, we thought pictures of the ingredient amounts could be easier to follow."

"Good thinking, Shawn. Graphs give pictures. If we let a line represent 58 points, we'll have a slightly shorter line to represent 56 points. If we use a circle to represent the total points scored, what happens? What do we need to do?" Mr. Prather paused for a few moments of thinking time, keeping track of how much time was passing to be sure he allowed enough time for the students to think.

"OK. Now with 3.7 seconds of silent indoor thinking completed, John, tell us how many total points were scored by the two teams combined."

"Um, 114, I think."

"Right. Now, Katie, please come up to the board and draw a big circle."

Katie followed that instruction. She asked, "Now what?"

"Good question. How can we make that circle into a graph or a picture showing the total points of 114, the 58 points from one team and the 56 points from the other team? Who has an idea Katie can use?"

John did. "Take the green marker and draw a line kind of like a diameter. Well, draw a radius first. Yeah. Now draw a second radius, but don't make it go straight from the other radius. We don't want a diameter because that would divide the circle in equal parts."

"Who can see the idea that John and Katie are coming up with?" Mr. Prather asked. "Let's put it into words. Write on your paper the words that describe this circle graph idea. Take one minute."

Tasha had an answer that impressed Mr. Prather, who looked at several answers as he walked around the room, "The circle is all of the points. The left part of the circle is a little bigger than half and is the 58 points. The right part is the 56 points." Tasha read her answer aloud.

Justin and Raphael asked if they could read their answers. Each answer included use of more colors in the circle to make a better graph. Mr. Prather asked Justin and Raphael to both draw their ideas on the board. The result was a circle with slightly more than half colored in green and slightly less than half colored in red. The idea was reinforced as the eraser was used to erase part of the green side to reveal the number 58 and part of the red side to reveal the number 56.

"Very clever and very colorful; the idea is becoming very clear. Graphs give us a picture to help show differences in numbers and to help us interpret numbers. Who has a question, insight or conclusion?"

Tasha did. "Is there any number that cannot be shown in a graph?"

"Great question. Anybody think of a number or group of numbers that could not be shown in graph form?"

Jeremy raised his hand after a few seconds. "We did lots of graphing in computer class, you know, x and y. We had positive numbers and negative numbers. We even did three dimensions with the z line. So, I'd say that any number could be graphed in one way or another."

(Author's note to the reader: Think of the difference in Mr. Prather's class if he had started class this way: "OK, turn to page 66. Read pages 66–70. Answer the questions on page 70 with complete sentences. When you finish that, we will discuss your answers. The homework for tomorrow is to read pages 71–75." Sure, the book may have worthwhile content, but the book does not teach; the book alone cannot cause real, extreme learning.)

"Good answer." Mr. Prather began to write some numbers on the overhead projector. "Now, let's make a mental move from the scoreboards you've drawn and the charts you've created to these numbers I'm putting on the overhead projector for you to see on the front screen. Take a few moments to make some sense out of these columns of statistics."

He allowed the class 10 seconds of silent indoor thinking—yes, 10 seconds of silence in a classroom could feel like 10 minutes, but great thinking and big ideas took a little time. Thoreau was right: "There is more to life than increasing its speed." For Jason Prather, there was more to teaching than increasing its speed. Ten seconds of thinking now could multiply into much learning later. Allowing only two seconds of thinking now may save eight seconds, he thought, but may deprive the class of eight big ideas that would have been created if students had been given more time to reflect, ponder, wonder, analyze, reason and think.

"OK, what is this chart about? Raphael, what do you think?"

"I think it shows how much money people make in their jobs."

"Right. What else does it show?"

"Well," Raphael continued, "I'm not sure. Something about school, I guess."

"Right again. The chart shows how much money people make in their jobs on average and matches that with how many years people went to school. Are there any conclusions you can make from these statistics?"

Justin knew. "Looks like more school equals more money, but that's not always true. Entertainers or athletes may not finish college, but they can get rich."

"True, Justin. There are exceptions. These numbers show us the average income of all people who dropped out of high school, who finished high school, who have some college experience, who finished college and who finished a graduate school degree. Generally, what do these numbers tell us happens as people get more education? Keisha?"

"They make more money," Keisha said.

"You're right. Now, what explains this? Why do college graduates usually make more money than high school graduates? Is it because they are older? It is because of something else?"

Mary Anne raised her hand. "You know how some companies are. They only interview people who went to college. So college helps you get the interview. Some of us in this room know more about computers than some college graduates know. I could do computer work now. Why won't they hire me?"

Mr. Prather knew this question was not about graphs, but it was an important and genuine question. "Mary Anne, let's find out. I'll call some people who work in computer businesses in our town and have them visit our class. Maybe on the day we go to the computer lab to do graph work we could have one of those people visit us. We'll get your questions answered by an expert soon. OK?" She nodded and smiled yes.

"Now, you've seen these statistics about years of school and average income. Please work together in your groups of three and create a graph that communicates the same statistics. A bar graph, a circle or other formats can work. You've got three minutes for this." While the groups of students worked, Jason monitored. He provided encouragement, praise, answers, questions, guidance and correction. The students knew the routine. At the end of three minutes, one student from each group put the group's work on the marker board. The board was soon filled with eight graphs, and Mr. Prather told each student to look at all eight graphs to find the basic idea of each graph. The students were also to see how the graphs were similar or different.

What followed was called a lightning round. Every student would give an answer out loud. Mr. Prather's statement was "Give us one observation, conclusion, idea, similarity or difference from the graphs. Be precise and be brilliant."

David: "More school. More salary."

James: "Staying in school can pay off."

Stewart: "Companies hire smart people."

Raphael: "It's worth it apparently to continue your education."

Marian: "Do whatever it takes to go to college."

Brittany: "The averages say that more education means more salary, but averages cover up some exceptions."

Kelly: "The charts are precise with numbers, but the graphs with bars or circles or lines really show the differences."

Thomas: "I need to make much better grades."

Tasha: "The circle graphs with wedges representing numbers can really help make a point if different colors are used."

Jeremy: "All my ideas have been said. I guess, you know, the best jobs usually go with the most education."

Angel: "Graphs are better for making presentations. Our graphs on the board look a lot better than a bunch of numbers and stuff would look."

Mary Anne: "All the charts and graphs have the same information. We just changed the format."

Keisha: "Graphs are easier to make with computers than when we draw them."

Shawn: "Working in a group created more ideas than working alone."

Kim: "I never thought of graduate school. I guess I'll have to. What is it?"

Martina: "I want to know more about these numbers. Where did they come from? How do we know they are right?"

John: "There needs to be a new format for graphs. Bar and circle graphs are very 20th-century pictures."

Justin: "We need laptops and smart boards to use instead of pencil and paper or the marker board. It would be more precise."

Adam: "Some people do well without college. These graphs don't tell about individual people. I guess these numbers are about big groups of typical people. Who wants to be typical?"

Joy: "What's left to say? I think our group made a good graph because we designed in on an x/y axis system to be scientific."

Heather: "It seems that high school is worth more effort than I thought, since getting to college is based on good work in high school."

Katie: "I agree. You know, money talks and people with more education must get more money."

Devin: "Mr. Prather, going last is tough. I'll just say that everyone else did great and I learned from them, OK?"

Mr. Prather laughed and, as Devin expected, required an answer. "Devin, try again. Keep thinking."

Devin: "Well, the graphs with green and yellow look better than graphs with any other colors. How's that?"

"That's fine, Devin. Great thinking by everyone. Now, you've gone from the scoreboard you drew to the statistics you put into graph form.

You've worked individually and in groups. I'm handing out the typical newspaper summary of high school basketball game statistics. It shows typical numbers: two-point and three-point shots made and attempted, fouls, turnovers, free throws and scores by quarter. Your job is to create five different graphs presenting the various data that are given. For example, if the summary has 15 out of 20 free throws hit, but you change that to 75 percent, that's fine. We have eight minutes left in class. Let's all get started now. Ask me questions if you need help. You can probably get half of this done now. For tomorrow you'll turn in the five graphs you designed. If you do this on a computer that's fine for up to three of the five graphs, but do at least two by hand first, so you can really see and feel the workings of a graph being made and so you can contrast or compare the by-hand and by-computer processes.

Mr. Prather's lesson on use of graphs to present information began with each student drawing a scoreboard. This built upon their knowledge of, experience with, interest in and skills in activities that typically include a scoreboard. This did not rely on a textbook. This relied on creative use of existing knowledge, interests and skills. Some students draw better than others. Some students like to draw more than others do. Still, drawing a scoreboard is a student-friendly activity that helped Mr. Prather's students to connect prior knowledge with the new knowledge coming through that day's lesson. It also helped connect school with life outside of school wherever scoreboards exist. It also created the possibility of quick success for each student. "I don't know the answer" or "I don't have my book" were not likely responses to the opening thought-starter activity in class that day.

Every student was involved in the thought starter. Every student was involved in the small group work. Every student participated in the lightning round. One of the extremes in Extreme Teaching is that every student is involved continuously in formal ways that are easily measured—drawing, answering a question, working in a group—and in informal ways such as paying attention closely.

Each student will now get started on the homework and will be able to do the homework. The amount of homework to be done is limited. The students need some practice with graph making and the data interpretation and/or data presentation involved in graph making; however, they do not need to complete graphs of the odd-numbered problems 7–41 on pages 67 and 68, for example. Use real statistics from a high school basketball game and students will see the importance, value and meaning of making or using graphs far more meaningfully than if the generic, distant, neutral topics of textbook pages about graphs are used. Students are real. Odd-numbered problems on pages 67 and 68 in a textbook are not real. By getting extremely real with students, teachers can help give students an extra reason to get really dedicated to learning at school.

The Extreme Teaching activity had much interaction between (a) students and students, (b) students and the teacher and (c) students, the teacher and ideas. That interaction can take classroom thinking and learning to extremes that worksheets and textbook activities can never see or reach. Textbooks and worksheets are finite and usually serve very finite, limited, minute purposes. The knowledge, interests and skills or talents of students are infinite. Extreme Teaching connects the infinite of what students bring to class with the infinite that students still have to learn and creates an energetic, dynamic, symbiotic process of connections between both of those infinities.

Mr. Prather had a video clip of the final few seconds of a basketball game, but he decided not to use it at this time with this class. Why? The scene on the video clip was finite and might have become the one right answer. The imagination of the students about what might happen during the final few seconds was more effective. Socrates was right—give students the right question and they can discover, find, invent and confirm the good answers a teacher seeks, and sometimes a better answer than the teacher expected.

Mr. Prather teaches from a foundation of essential convictions about and extreme ideals about teaching. Here's what he requires of himself day after day as an Extreme Teacher.

The Ideals of an Extreme Teacher

1. Extreme Teachers do more. Extreme teachers do better. Extreme teachers give 110 percent.
2. Extreme Teachers think, reflect and conclude.
3. Extreme Teachers listen.

4. Extreme Teachers learn.
5. Extreme Teachers create opportunities for students to succeed.
6. Extreme Teachers believe that to every problem there is an equal and opposite solution.
7. Extreme Teachers accept this standard for themselves: results, not excuses. Extreme teachers require students to follow that same standard.
8. Extreme Teachers follow great examples. Extreme teachers set a great example.
9. Extreme Teachers speak selectively, purposefully and precisely, knowing that every thought that enters the brain should not necessarily exit from the mouth.
10. Extreme Teachers cause learning.

Jason Prather's school district would make some progress during the year following the start of the new plan to increase test scores. The demographic education training was later conducted by expensive consultants who probably meant well, were conscientious and did their best, but there was no convincing evidence that different groups of students needed to be taught differently due to their demographic descriptions. Teaching methods can be varied due to academic strengths or academic needs of students, but that is determined by performance, not demographics. School district data showed that every demographic group had high achievers, moderate achievers and low achievers. Case closed.

Anyway, Extreme Teaching accounts for demographic differences and all other differences. When Extreme Teachers take an inventory or survey of their students' knowledge, interests, talents and skills, those teachers identify what to connect new learning with. That was true for Socratic teaching as presented by Plato. That is true for Extreme Teaching as presented by Jason Prather.

Well-intentioned community members and educators, or seriously mistaken social engineers who seek to lead teachers into a scheme of teaching students from different demographics in different ways because of their demographics—gender, ethnicity, socioeconomic status or other factors—may intentionally raise constitutional issues based on the Fourteenth Amendment and on the 1954 *Brown vs. The Board of*

Education decision by the U.S. Supreme Court. Dr. Martin Luther King's dream was for his children to be judged by the content of their character, not by the color of their skin. Applied to teaching, King's dream calls for teaching to be based on a starting point not centered on demographics but on the content of what each student knows, is interested in, and is good at and to build upon that foundation to make connections with what needs to be learned now.

The two new central office positions Jason's school district created lasted only one year. One of the TEST coordinators moved to another school district, and the other became a high school assistant principal. The vacant positions were not filled, and, as no one in the district indicated a need for the services provided by TEST coordinators, the positions were abolished.

Most schools in the district showed improvement on the next round of state tests. Jason's school showed the second highest gain in the district. This was especially encouraging, because Jason's school was already much higher than the school that improved more. Jason's school raised its score from 71 to 75. The other school moved from 46 to 54. Both schools reached their goals, but the challenge to improve is greater at the higher end of the scale, which goes to 100.

So, the school district did decide to use Extreme Teaching in all schools. Would that solve all of their problems? No. There is no one solution to all of education's problems. But would Extreme Teaching give teachers and students a fascinating way to cause learning? Yes. When learning is caused, students benefit and increase their commitment to school. Teachers benefit and see more career satisfaction. And what about test scores? When all of that happens, they go up.

CHAPTER 5

Extreme Teaching: Thoughts, Hopes

Jason Prather spent a lot of time thinking about school. School today is different. School, Jason concluded, will never again be what some experienced educators think it used to be. Schools have increasingly changed from places where everyone could attend, but where some students would learn much, some students would learn little and other students would drop out. School today, for good or bad, is increasingly a full social services center where everything from education to food, health care to clothing, day care to dispensing medicine, housing to transportation, psychological help to conflict mediation, juvenile court liaisons to child abuse investigations, court-ordered attendance to doctor-ordered accommodations are more and more common. School today is not what school was a decade ago or a generation ago. School today is different.

So, what's a teacher to do? Jason has asked himself that question with a blunt, personal level of introspection that he had not expected. What is a teacher supposed to do so that every student learns, so that every difficult or nearly impossible special education accommodation is made in one classroom while every proper challenge is simultaneously given to gifted or talented students? Jason knew he was a very good teacher; sometimes he was a great teacher. He expected near perfection from himself, so even on his very good or great days he could still feel frustration, disappointment or worse. In the worst moments, Jason seriously asked himself if he should consider other work. His heart and soul and mind were in the classroom, but teaching now had become a very different job than the work Jason prepared for in college, in volunteer duties at church camps, at tutoring programs he helped with on Saturdays when he was in high school. Teaching is different; school is different. What's a capable, conscientious teacher to do? Jason knew that Extreme Teaching showed him what to do for designing instruction and for causing learning. Still, he wondered, for the part of a teacher's work that impacts his or her own heart, soul, mind, body and health, was there some Extreme Advice or Extreme Encouragement available?

Jason wrote his thoughts on paper. For Jason Prather, the answer to "What's a teacher to do?" had usually been "Work harder, work more hours, say yes to more duties before school or after school." Jason wondered if he had just reached the limit of what one teacher's heart, soul, mind and body could endure. He knew that teaching was the only work for him, but teaching had changed. He believed in Extreme Teaching, yet he felt some extreme demands that could sometimes begin to exhaust him. What caused this unexpected bout with discouragement? A test caused it.

The test Jason gave to this class followed two weeks of every teaching method Jason knew of that could possibly cause learning. The test results were 10 A grades, 5 B grades, 5 C grades, 4 D grades and 3 F grades. Yes, more students made A or B grades than made lower grades. Yes, the overall class grade was good. Still, 12 students made a C or lower. Questions that students missed were not difficult. If Jason had made any further adjustments to the teaching and testing process to assist or to accommodate students further, it would have been difficult to call the process education. When the work is all but done for the student, is that really teaching and learning?

So, Jason put his thoughts on paper. He decided to write 100 inspirational, creative, encouraging, insightful or challenging thoughts. This would give him one thought to read to himself at school each day of the first semester of the year. He would then read the same thoughts in sequence, one each day, during the second semester of the school year.

What's a teacher to do? Think and hope. Jason put his thinking and his hopes on paper so he could provide some Extreme Teaching to himself. He decided that a variety would be most helpful, so some thoughts are written in first person and others in different voices, including Jason sometimes taking a third-person view of himself, but the voices are all from deep and honorable convictions.

SCHOOL THOUGHT 1

It's worth it. Teaching is worth it. Despite the frustrations and the disappointments. Despite the endless work hours to grade papers or to prepare lessons or to attend meetings. Despite the defiant, lazy, disruptive students who are determined to fail when their brain power is more than sufficient for success. Despite homework not turned in. Despite procedures, policies, laws and regulations that serve bureaucratic or political goals. Despite school boards, state legislators, governors, members of Congress and presidents who act as if legislation can educate students. Despite narrow-minded interest groups lobbying for preferential treatment. Despite adults who make excuses for students. Despite students who lie, cheat, defy, curse, threaten, steal, fight and terrorize. Despite difficulties that have not been invented yet but that are certain to emerge.

Teaching is still worth it. Why? Because of Kelly and Jared, because of Michelle and Owen, because of Julie and Brian, because of Katie and Robert. Because when you put a name with a face and realize anew that it is what can happen today in your classroom that could ignite a spark of thinking and of inspiration in the mind of young Samantha, who learns something today and who decides it is worth her effort to learn more tomorrow, then it is all worth it.

Teachers count time in years: it is your first year of teaching; it is your twentieth year of teaching. Yet, teachers teach in moments. At the moment when class begins today, the teacher can fascinate students or can just pass the time with students.

The potential for each student to become fascinated and for each moment to be a time of classroom fascination makes teaching worth it.

More than that, students are worth it. The continued hope of human life to improve with each generation requires that students today be taught magnificently. To be part of that honorable and nearly impossible adventure is to live a life that matters. Teaching matters because students matter. Teaching is worth it because students are worth it.

SCHOOL THOUGHT 2

What's the biggest problem in education? Perhaps it is those adults who do not do their jobs.

Today there are five teachers absent at school. They are not facing emergencies; that has been confirmed. Whatever they allegedly needed to do today could have been done last weekend or during the last vacation. It's too early for the flu season. This semester just began yesterday, but five teachers stayed home.

I sometimes wonder if I should work less than I do. I've taken three sick days in my years of teaching. I arrive at school early, and I stay late. I come in on weekends, or I work at home on school duties for many hours during weekends. There are easier ways, there are shortcuts, and there are compromises. All of these are taken daily by some educators who are not violating a law and who still get paid in full. They let videos fill the time in class. They live at the copy machine, pushing buttons to make more copies of nearly worthless, very generic, painfully dull and pointless worksheets and tests provided by textbook publishers. That is not teaching. A minimum wage clerk can copy workbook pages, distribute those to students, collect them and grade them! That same clerk can show a video. Real teachers do more. Real teachers come to work and are prepared to cause learning, are devoted to causing learning and are eager to cause learning.

Five teachers are absent today for no good reason. May their conscience bother them. Thank you to everyone else who did come to school today.

I'm here today. My students are here today. In my classroom, learning will be caused. To do less is unethical, unprofessional and unacceptable, even if doing less is legal and is tolerated. Rather than resent people who "steal" their pay because of having done little work, I will teach magnificently. I cannot make those five teachers become responsible, but I can take my responsibilities seriously and I can teach my students effectively. I will put my energy toward what I can control. I will teach, and the experience for students in my classroom will be wonderful. Maybe those five absent teachers do not realize what they are missing.

SCHOOL THOUGHT 3

Success. The students were given their first test yesterday, which was the second day of school. I graded the papers last night. Every student made an A or B grade. That was the intention. They now know that success is possible.

The students were not told that they would have a test yesterday, but tests are given in my class whenever tests are the best way to teach. Based on what we did in class the first day of the semester and on what I am confident they already know, the test presented no difficulty to any student who would think, write and draw.

To each returned test was taped a penny. They now know that I will pay them for working. That is very capitalistic. It is a small amount of money, but it really intrigues the students. It invites a great discussion. It causes learning. It confirms that I value them and their work. It creates good memories. It inspires. It amuses. It stands out. It is one of those creative opportunities teachers have to boldly touch lives and minds. It is one reason that students look forward to tests in this class. Imagine that. "Mr. Prather, could we please have another test?"

SCHOOL THOUGHT 4

"You should be a school administrator. You'd be a great principal." Jason Prather was hearing these words again from a well-meaning colleague. Jason replied politely.

"I'm a teacher. I always intended to be a teacher. That has not changed. I thrive on direct academic interaction with students in the classroom. Take me out of the classroom and you take the air out of my lungs or the blood out of my heart. I'm a teacher."

Jason's colleague was surprised. "So dramatic, Professor Prather."

Jason agreed. "You're right. Teachers get to be part of the moment-to-moment adventurous drama of students learning, of students growing up, of students enduring trials and errors, of students becoming—we hope—the ideal that life has in mind for them."

Jason appreciates the demanding work, the ruthless schedule and the endless ordeals that school administrators experience. Jason teaches because Jason is a teacher, 100 percent. Being a school administrator is a very different job than being a schoolteacher. Jason does what stirs his heart, mind and soul. Jason teaches.

SCHOOL THOUGHT 5

There is a sign in Jason Prather's classroom: "You are now entering a Results, Not Excuses zone." Over the years the students have accepted the reality that Mr. Prather lives up to the standard of "Results, Not Excuses" and that they must also live up to that standard.

Jason convinced students years ago that Results, Not Excuses would rule his classroom. A homework assignment was due on Wednesday. Jason had given students almost one week to complete the work. On the due date, 10 of 27 students had nothing to turn in. The next day, Jason returned the homework to the 17 students who had completed it on time. On that Thursday, he gave every student a new homework assignment for Friday. The Friday homework was real and was educational, but it was a very short task that could easily be completed in 15 minutes. Jason provided about 10 minutes of class time for students to begin the homework.

For the 10 students who had turned in nothing on Wednesday, their grade was zero, and their Friday assignment included two separate parts: the new 15-minute task, plus the original homework that had been due on Wednesday. It was due again, this time on Friday, and it was a longer assignment this time.

"That's not fair. We have two assignments," one student complained.

"You're right. It's not fair that you are making me do the extra work of assigning again homework that you should have already done. The only way to make this assignment go away is to do it completely, correctly and on schedule." Jason spoke with the certainty of a unanimous Supreme Court decision.

Two students did not turn in the homework on Friday. It was due for them on Monday. Jason stopped by their homes early on Saturday morning to visit their parents/guardians and to wake up the students. (He had prearranged this with the support of their families). The work was turned in on Monday.

"Mr. Prather will wake you up on Saturday if you don't do your homework. Just go ahead and get it done." Students spread the word. Another victory for Results, Not Excuses.

SCHOOL THOUGHT 6

"You are entering a worksheet-free zone" is another sign in Mr. Prather's classroom. Jason does create thinksheets, which students use to compile information, ideas, analyses, reflections, connections and applications. Jason never uses prepared, off-the-shelf, generic, anonymous worksheets made by distant strangers who do not know his students. Jason also does not fall for technology tricks: An old-fashioned, worthless, generic paper worksheet put on a website or a compact disc is still generic and worthless.

Does it take more time for Jason to create all the materials for his classes to use each year? No, because they work the first time. Jason's materials work better for him and for his students, so remedial work is usually minimal or is eliminated altogether. The generic materials cause busywork; they do not cause learning.

When Jason Prather's students use the materials he prepares for them, no student has to wonder, "What do they mean with question 10?" The students ask, "Mr. Prather, what do you mean with question 10?" The interaction is real, is personal, is worthwhile and is one more step in the learning journey. The students are being led on this journey by their teacher, but the students are very active participants.

SCHOOL THOUGHT 7

Drill and practice. Drill and practice. Drill and practice. These activities are completely acceptable as part of a total learning program.

Old-fashioned spelling tests have merit. Memorizing the multiplication table through 12 x 12 has merit. Memorizing the Preamble to the Constitution and memorizing the Gettysburg Address are great mental exercises. Drill and practice can work; higher-order thinking skills need a solid foundation of fundamental thinking skills.

The age of an idea is not in itself a reason to use or reject the idea. Does the idea work; does it get the desired results in a good way? If so, use it. If not, use another idea.

Drill and practice can cause learning. Somewhere between never using drill and practice and always using drill and practice is a reasonable amount. Use drill and practice when it is the best way to cause the intended learning.

SCHOOL THOUGHT 8

An achievement gap is the difference between the current knowledge and the skills of each and of every student versus the knowledge and skills that each and every student can master.

The achievement gap can be addressed and resolved for each individual student. Teachers educate individual students who attend classes in groups of 20 or 25 to 30 or so. Teachers do not educate demographic data. A headline stating an achievement gap between one demographic group and another demographic group is a misleading headline.

Group A 13-year-olds read at a 74 level. Group B 13-year-olds read at a 63 level. Fix the gap, now! But an overall number for the reading level of Group A or Group B tells nothing about any individual student in Group A or Group B. Cause each and every student to learn, and achievement gaps fade away. Structure the achievement gap debate with a demographic basis, and everyone loses because education gets lost in the political battles or the inflamed rhetoric of interest groups with varied motives. Group A does not learn to read. Real students, one at a time, learn to read.

SCHOOL THOUGHT 9

Teach students how to be great students. Major American corporations spend much money to train adult employees on skills such as time management, effective meeting practices, effective communication, creativity or teamwork. If adult workers benefit from training in these skills so they can excel at their work, it is reasonable that students also can benefit from training in the mechanics of being a great student.

Do students know how to take notes, organize papers so the papers are where they should be when they are due, schedule study time so work is done regularly, get to class on time, prepare for a test, research a topic or take various types of exams?

Football coaches do not say to teams, "Go out and score points." Coaches divide football into many precise, separate skills that are practiced, practiced and practiced.

Teachers should not say "study and learn." Rather, students benefit from being shown how to divide studying and learning into many precise, separate skills and actions that are practiced, practiced, practiced, evaluated, evaluated, evaluated, improved, improved, improved, rewarded, rewarded, rewarded.

SCHOOL THOUGHT 10

"When will we ever need to know algebra?"

"When will we ever need to know what Shakespeare said?"

"When will we need to know anything about a noun?"

"I'm not going to be an artist. Why do I have to take an art class?"

Those are valid questions from students. The students deserve to be shown how learning at school today connects with their real lives today. Jason Prather uses Extreme Teaching to accomplish that.

Jason also asks this question: "How many of you expect to spend much time after graduating from high school tackling people? Will you tackle your college professors or your manager at work or the clerk at a store where you buy something?"

The students usually get the point. Football, something they get very excited about, teaches the skill of tackling, which will be used in their lives less than algebra, Shakespeare, nouns or art.

SCHOOL THOUGHT 11

Discipline whenever necessary.

Reward whenever possible.

Teach at all times.

When students misbehave, they need to know that their actions were wrong and that what they did was bad. Vague words such as "inappropriate" or rationalizations such as "you made an improper choice" are superficial, evasive and inaccurate. Wrong is clear. Bad is clear. When students are wrong or bad in their behavior they need a penalty or a punishment, not a "consequence" that is one more vague, empty, politically correct or psychologically correct meaningless word.

We get more of what we reward. But usually, for students who behave well, the benefit is simply not getting punished. Wait a minute. If I misbehave I get punished, but if I behave I just get to avoid punishment. That equation is not balanced. We get more of what we reward. The most valuable and the most acclaimed recognition at a school should be for academic achievement, and the second most significant category to acknowledge is great behavior and citizenship at school.

Marching bands and athletic teams deserve cheers, assemblies and trophies. Students who achieve in academics and/or in proper behavior deserve more cheers, more assemblies and more trophies. What we reward reveals our true priorities.

We are always able to teach. When discipline is imposed, there can be a learning moment created. When rewards are given, students can learn what is valued and how to gain rewards. Every action at a school teaches something. The goal is to be sure that what should be taught is taught. If we overlook misbehavior, we teach that misbehavior is accepted. If we cheer touchdowns or home runs but not academic accomplishments, we teach that sports matters more than classes. When teachers who also coach demand more from students in athletics than from students in academics, the wrong message is sent. When more work and publicity are given to filling a coaching vacancy than to filling a teaching vacancy, the wrong message is sent. The students are always watching.

SCHOOL THOUGHT 12

Beware of trends and fads. Measure ideas against this standard: Is learning caused effectively and efficiently?

Learning styles. Culturally sensitive curriculum. Differentiated instruction. Brain-based research. Education reform. High-stakes test. National curriculum.

Maybe a national curriculum could be used to cause some learning, but a curriculum from the U.S. Department of Education is less effective and is less efficient than curriculum work done at the state and local levels.

Schools cannot just chase the idea, fad or trend of this month and add that to last month's idea, fad or trend.

A solid teaching method that incorporates many ideas is effective and efficient. A solid teaching method that energizes and instructs students while providing rewarding career experiences for teachers makes sense. Resist the temptation to desperately grab a trend, fad or idea. Teach. Cause learning. Teach extremely. Cause extreme learning.

SCHOOL THOUGHT 13

After all the education reforms are reformed yet again, after all the education laws are updated again, after all the standardized test scores are debated again, after all the acts of Congress to help education are reauthorized, after every state legislature and governor sets new goals for schools, after school boards revise old policies again, after civic groups and interest groups squeeze their agendas into schools, education still boils down to what happens or does not happen between teachers and students in classrooms. It is the teaching that matters more than any of the other variables that educators or others who seek to change schools can impact. It's the teaching. For Extreme Teachers, that truth is very good news.

SCHOOL THOUGHT 14

Pay very little attention to news media stories about education. It is likely that most reporters who do stories about education are assigned to that topic briefly and develop no solid expertise about education. It is also likely that media groups put an emphasis on education stories to appeal to a hidden motive.

Extreme Teachers have one dominant motive: to cause learning by making meaningful and fascinating connections between what students know, are interested in and/or are good at and with what students need to know, be interested in and/or be good at. The teacher's job is to teach. The modern media's job is to uncover the next Watergate. Just keep teaching with the certainty that almost every media obsession is replaced soon by the next media obsession.

SCHOOL THOUGHT 15

Students have the responsibility to do the work that teachers have designed to be meaningful, useful, fascinating, worthwhile, interactive and connected.

Parents and guardians have the responsibility to not make excuses for students. "Well, he was so busy last night I told him not to worry about the homework. It's really my fault."

Teachers hope that students and parents and guardians accept their responsibilities, but in any case, teachers are still required to do their duty to cause learning.

SCHOOL THOUGHT 16

"Do the odd-numbered problems on page 63 for tomorrow. Get started now."

It is a strong tribute to students that they resist the temptation to respond, "You know, all of the problems on page 63 are odd." They would be right. The typical page 63 in the typical math book has utterly useless problems about two trains leaving the station or about the ages of two unknown people whose years lived have some algebraic relation to each other, but who has ever said, "Guess what? Today is my birthday and I'm two times my sister's age, but $\frac{1}{3}$ my mother's age. How old am I?"

Create real math problems that relate to the real lives that students are living now so they see that math is real, not odd.

SCHOOL THOUGHT 17

How a teacher thinks about teaching impacts how a teacher teaches. Some people would suggest that teachers should think of teaching as facilitating learning, which means to create experiences that give students the opportunity to learn. Other people insist that the purpose of teaching is to cause learning, which is to do whatever is necessary—within proper limits of law, ethics, professional conduct, policies and procedures—to make learning happen.

A teacher who thinks of teaching as facilitating learning could say, "I taught them, but they did not learn." That seems similar to a car manufacturer saying "We built the cars, but they just won't run" or a restaurant manager saying "We cooked the food, but nobody could stomach it." How silly it sounds to say, "I facilitated the students, but they still failed."

Teachers who think of teaching as causing learning say, "I taught them; therefore, they learned." When real teaching happens, learning happens. If learning did not occur, there may have been much work, labor, effort and time put into the task, but it cannot be called teaching.

SCHOOL THOUGHT 18

"You really made a difference to me. Thanks for being my teacher. I needed your help and you were there. You never would let me quit. Thanks. I hated it then, but I appreciate it now."

"Middle school is easy. You really prepared me."

"High school is not as hard as I expected. You really prepared me."

"College is difficult, but I can do it. You really prepared me."

Put a dollar value on those comments from former students and it becomes clear that teachers are given priceless compensation. Sure, everyone wants higher salaries, but teachers can get some pay that money cannot touch, because teachers can touch lives.

SCHOOL THOUGHT 19

"If you would behave better in this class, we could do something interesting." The teacher spoke sincerely, yet with a frustration that had been accumulating. She would like to provide creative, hands-on, enjoyable, active experiences in the classroom for her students, but until they got themselves under control and did the assignments she gave them—read each section of chapter 6 in the book and answer the questions at the end of each section, plus the chapter review questions at the end—how could she trust them to do anything less structured?

Several students thought in response to the teacher: "If we did something interesting in class, we would behave better."

There is a symbiotic solution. Teaching in ways that inspire students to work, to think, to learn and to cooperate will create rewarding career experiences for teachers. Typical worksheets and ordinary questions in a chapter do very little for students or for teachers. Students are energetic, creative and interactive. Asking students to sit down, be still and be quiet from age 5 to age 18 just will not work. Connect with the strengths, interests, skills and knowledge of students. School does not need to become an amusement park or an entertainment center. People who are age 5–18 will learn continuously throughout their childhood and teenage years. When those students are not at school, they are often active, energetic, vibrant, interactive and involved. They learn by seeing, hearing, doing, thinking, talking, watching, interacting, reading, experiencing and more. They seek that which fascinates, explains, intrigues and compels. No other part of life for people aged 5–18 expects them to sit still, be quiet and follow pedantic routines that are less challenging, invigorating and worthwhile than students are able to appreciate.

Students who are fascinated by activities at school become students who are dedicated to school. That dedication can help prevent misbehavior or apathy.

Teachers who provide fascinating activities at school for students are teachers who will have rewarding, interactive and personal learning experiences with students. Everyone wins when this happens.

SCHOOL THOUGHT 20

Teachers are people. Students are people. This common peopleness can be a great resource for school success. How? Read on, please.

Beware of bureaucracy. Laws, rules, policies and procedures are necessary for the order, predictability and guidance they provide; however, laws, rules, policies and procedures do not teach students: teachers teach students. Teachers are real people living real lives right now. Their teaching career is a significant part of the hours they live daily. Students are real people who are living real lives right now. Their experiences and time at school are significant parts of the lives they live daily.

Make school real, genuine, humane, interactive, personal, interpersonal, caring, vibrant, demanding, challenging, fascinating, purposeful, active, probing, full of wonder, discovery, curiosity and adventure. Put your heart, mind and soul into school so school can put some invigoration back into your heart, mind and soul.

The purpose of a school is to cause learning of, by and for people and of, by and for the real lives those people—students and teachers—are all living today and will live for many tomorrows.

SCHOOL THOUGHT 21

When a large corporation in the United States decides to change a product it makes, the process involves research, engineering and manufacturing. The design of a bottle is changed to be easier to grip. The fragrance of a detergent is changed in response to consumer research that indicated a new preference. The body of a car is changed to incorporate scientific progress and cosmetic appeal. After all the research, engineering and manufacturing changes are made, the new product appears and the old product is replaced.

Some political, business, community and interest group leaders seem frustrated that schools cannot be changed through the same process that corporations and consumer products use for change. Manufacturing processes are far more controllable via implementation of decisions by corporate officers than are education processes. When a state law is passed that changes how education is to be provided, the thousands of human variables that exist in each school bring complexities and complications that surpass those of any corporation's production processes.

What can educators do about a citizenry or a school board that thinks of schools as corporations, thinks that they can simply give the directive to change the product and the product will be changed? It can speak up and give those well-meaning citizens and school board members a lesson in reality. Begin by inviting them to visit the school for a week. Corporate leaders who accurately know their company and know their competitive arena get out of their offices and go into the factories, research laboratories, marketplace and consumer research sessions to learn for themselves what the current business reality is.

Those people who could claim any knowledge about what school reality is, what needs to improve at schools or how to improve schools must have been in classrooms, school hallways and other parts of schools to see reality recently and often. Those people could add to their insight and legitimacy by substitute teaching occasionally—this idea also applies to school district employees who work at a central office or have other support duties that are not carried out in schools.

Schools are not corporations, and schools are not manufacturing products.

Schools are people places where what is produced—learning—is interactively and interpersonally caused, not automatically or mechanically manufactured.

SCHOOL THOUGHT 22

We know what works. There is much comfort in that truth. Educators are not cast into their schools and classrooms without sources of ideas or solutions.

The student who does no work in one class may do superior work in another class. The group of students who misbehave daily with one teacher in one classroom may behave perfectly each day with a different teacher who teaches a different subject in a different room. The variable is not the subject matter or the classroom location. The variable is what is done and how it is done, both by the teacher and the students.

Teachers can learn a lot from each other. To every problem there is an equal and opposite solution. For the major problem in your classroom, another teacher down the hall may have discovered a solution. Far too often, educators do not share their success stories or trade ideas.

We know what works. No one teacher knows everything that works, but he or she can find out by asking, listening, watching, reading, researching and exploring.

SCHOOL THOUGHT 23

Think of the best teachers you ever had. Think deeply and clearly of exact moments in the classroom with those teachers. What did they do that worked so very well that it can be remembered precisely and fondly years later?

Now, do what those teachers did. No new laws, taxes, policies or regulations are needed. Just do what great teachers have shown you. Your students will benefit. Plus, years from now, when your students think of their best teachers, they will precisely and fondly remember you.

In other words, be better than the best teachers you ever had by using all of their exemplary skills, plus your talents. Be the great teacher you always wished that each and every one of your teachers had been. Be the great teacher you promised yourself you would be when you chose teaching as a career or when teaching chose you.

SCHOOL THOUGHT 24

When people are asked to think of the best teachers they ever had and are then asked to explain what those teachers did that stands out so favorably, the answers are usually as follows:

- They cared about me.
- They made learning interesting.
- They really liked what they were doing.
- They took extra time with me.
- They challenged me.
- They knew what they were talking about.
- They were excited and enthusiastic.
- They showed us how learning related to our lives.

What's the common thread in those responses? Great teachers are remembered because of their people skills and their academic competence. One without the other is failure. Both together can positively touch a life forever.

SCHOOL THOUGHT 25

There are drill and practice activities in which a teacher poses questions at fast-forward speed and students give instant answers. That pace serves a valid purpose. But when teachers ask a question that should stimulate some deeper thinking, reasoning, reflection and analysis— "What does Jefferson mean by 'inalienable rights'?"—students should be given a few seconds for silent thinking.

Recall of one bit of information can be instantaneous, but reflection on the meaning of an idea takes some time. Allow a few moments for students to think.

SCHOOL THOUGHT 26

Today, the students will be introduced to the idea that people once thought the earth was flat. From this idea, the students and the teacher will explore and analyze other formerly held conclusions such as the one that the sun moves around the Earth. For students who have always known that the Earth is round and that the Earth orbits the sun, the former beliefs of earlier centuries may be easily dismissed as prehistoric, laughable mistakes.

So, the teacher asks the students: "When you were very young, what did you think a bank did with money that people deposited there?"

The common answer, if students can accurately recall their perceptions of banks from early childhood, is usually "they put it in the big safe, locked it up and kept it until you came back for it." During the teenage and young adult years, the understanding of what a bank does with money transformed from that childish perspective to the actual understanding of financial reality.

Now, students may be able to see that people in earlier centuries were not intentionally wrong in their perspective, observations and conclusions about the Earth. The Earth looked flat to them. The sun sure acted as if it orbited the Earth, and that big safe in the bank must be where all of the money is locked securely. In the perception of many students, schoolwork can look very flat and motionless, when actually it should be vibrantly shaped and endlessly dynamic.

SCHOOL THOUGHT 27

Great teaching is exhausting. When done with all of the effort and energy required, great teaching wears out the most devoted, dedicated, prepared, capable and enthusiastic teacher.

How do great teachers recharge their batteries so they can teach greatly again tomorrow after getting magnificently, joyfully, productively and intentionally exhausted today?

Be good to yourself. Take care of yourself. Do yourself some lovely favor before the day is out. Earned exhaustion from putting heart, mind, body and soul into great teaching is honorable; however, you need to be renewed in heart, mind, body and soul for tomorrow's great academic adventure.

Beginning tomorrow still exhausted from today would be unhealthy. Take good care of yourself. School is short—teach extremely. Life is short—live wisely.

SCHOOL THOUGHT 28

Students in elementary schools, middle schools and high schools are usually vibrant, energetic, curious, dynamic and adventurous. The many aspects of life that they are beginning to encounter can intrigue, fascinate, frighten, challenge, overwhelm, harm or enhance them. Looking at life from their youthful perspective can be revealing to teachers. Enabling students to look at life from a mature adult perspective can be educational for students. Both perspectives are genuine. The youthful perspective will probably fade over time into the adult perspective, as reality usually insists on having its way and the adult years bring responsibilities that force all but the most persistently youthful to conform to the duties of employee, family head, taxpayer and law-abiding citizen.

Yet the souls of young people—the energy, curiosity, wonder, enthusiasm, imagination, adventure and openness—need not be squelched in the name of rapidly transforming students into adults. Perhaps exposing the souls of young people to extreme educational experiences that build upon their energy, curiosity, wonder, enthusiasm, imagination, adventure and openness would cause those young people to apply more and better learning today as students and in later years as adults.

SCHOOL THOUGHT 29

When Plato, Aristotle and Socrates taught their students, few classroom materials were available. There were no machines to plug in. There were no technology-assisted instructional systems. There was a teacher; there were students; there were topics to master; there was wisdom of the ages to consider; there were thoughts to analyze; there were life experiences to evaluate; there were theories to probe; there were explanations to prove or disprove; and there was vibrant, interactive, profound discussion that journeyed to the essence of ideas, of people and of life.

The thoughts of Plato, Aristotle and Socrates were so powerful and beneficial and instructional that they are still read, pondered and prized today. Of course, teachers should still make use of genuine advances in teaching materials; however, learning can still be caused with just a teacher and some students relentlessly exploring a meaningful idea using their life experiences, their minds, their imagination, their questions and their answers.

SCHOOL THOUGHT 30

"That was unsmart." One student was overheard making that comment to another student. *Unsmart* is not a dictionary word, but *unsmart* made perfect sense to the student who said it and to the student who heard it. The other student had acted in a silly, childish, annoying way that was accurately described as unsmart. No debate or excuse followed; he knew that he had been unsmart.

Occasionally a student will use words that are not dictionary-approved, but assuming that the words pass a test of decency, it can be useful to initially express an adult idea in students' words. The more advanced and the more sophisticated vocabulary can follow, but if understanding is gained first by using words that make sense for students, then take advantage of that first step. Don't stop with the student word—take the students further and deeper into ideas that more complicated words can reveal—but be willing to start with words that are already meaningful to students. It could be unsmart to miss the opportunity for the students' vocabulary to be a teaching tool.

SCHOOL THOUGHT 31

When classroom activities connect with what students already know, are already good at and/or are already interested in, there is every reason to expect and to require more work and better work from students. Connecting with student knowledge, skills or interests does not mean to let students do only what comes easily or what seems to be enjoyable.

For students who are interested in cars, the new knowledge to be acquired is not limited to knowing more about the latest, most expensive, most sporty or coolest car. Rather, from the foundation of a student's knowledge of cars, skills in car maintenance, ability to drive (or desire to drive, if the student is not old enough yet) and interest in how a car functions, the connections can include all of the following:

- The industrial revolution, mass production, assembly lines.
- The physics and chemistry associated with fuel usage by internal combustion machines.
- The history of transportation.
- The math of buying a car and maintaining a car.
- Reading books about inventors, business leaders and race car drivers.
- Researching available information from a variety of sources about the ecological impact of automobile exhaust pollution.
- How laws are made and how different governmental jurisdictions—local, state, national—are involved in regulations about cars, roads, fuel and driving.
- International perspectives—how is driving regulated in other countries?
- Driver safety education.
- How computers are used in the manufacturing of, repair of and daily operation of cars.
- Sociology—what impact does the mobility that cars provide have on teenagers, families, workers, small communities, large cities and neighborhoods?

So, when students resist the current curriculum, surprise them by connecting their existing knowledge, skills and/or interests with that curriculum. Their prior knowledge is a reason to expect more work and to require better work.

Also, when students offer a typical excuse to not do work—"This is boring," "I can't do this," "I don't understand," "This isn't fun," "This is too hard,"—the teacher can very quickly negate the excuse by saying,

"Well, we're discussing what you said you were interested in, so you should be the expert on this topic," or "Everything we're doing today comes from what you said you were talented in; that means you should be showing all of us how this is done," or "I know that schoolwork can seem that way, but the survey I took of all students said that everyone knew something about sports, so every math problem we're doing today is about sports—you got exactly what you asked for. There really are no excuses, so show me some results."

SCHOOL THOUGHT 32

Teaching is not merely what the teacher does. Learning is not merely what the student does. Ideally, teachers and students are simultaneously, reciprocally and symbiotically learning together.

The students may be learning math while the teacher is learning what works best to cause the current students to master math.

The students may be sharing new insights, information or perspectives that the teacher did not know but that the students have researched for a class assignment.

Yes, the adult is in charge. Yes, the adults have more education and more life experience than the students. Yes, the adult is the teacher. Still, if the teacher and the students enter the classroom with a shared sense of wonder, fascination and eagerness to learn, there can be moments when everyone in the classroom is teaching and everyone in the classroom is learning.

SCHOOL THOUGHT 33

"What can we do to help our son/daughter do better at school?" There are many possible answers to this question that so many parents and guardians ask. Here's one answer: "Help your son or daughter see the connections between school and other parts of life." The exact activity may vary with the student's age, but imagine that a family is looking around the community for a new house to buy. The child or children in the family could be shown practical applications of math as mortgage payments and other calculations are made. The child or children could see which scientific ideas are included in the design and in the operational systems—heat, air conditioning, electricity, plumbing and appliances—of the house. A teenager could be shown the local government office where property transaction information is kept and could learn about local laws that impact property.

If the house buying example is too rare an event to use, give the teenager in the family the grocery list and a budget. See if he or she can manage the math and the economics.

SCHOOL THOUGHT 34

There is never enough time. Teachers have family responsibilities, personal obligations, duties at home, activities outside of school, chores to do, errands to run, doctor's appointments and all of the other common time-consuming tasks of daily life.

There is never enough time. Teachers have papers to grade, lessons to plan, conferences to attend, meetings with parents and guardians of students, faculty meetings, committee meetings, training sessions, professional development workshops, supervision duties, clubs to sponsor, teams to coach, more papers to grade and more lessons to plan, plus some new requirement from "them"—federal government, state government, local school board, a grant source of funding or another vague and faraway group—mandating that additional documentation about certain students be kept daily.

There is never enough time, so doing what is efficient and effective the first time is vital. First, talk to other teachers about what works well in their classrooms. Borrow the best teaching ideas and the best classroom management ideas. Second, continuously show students how the work at school relates to their prior knowledge, their existing skills and their current interests. With that connection made early, directly and often we can hope that students will learn more and will learn better, thereby minimizing or reducing failure and avoiding having to spend teacher time or student time on remedial work.

SCHOOL THOUGHT 35

If at all possible, school administrators should also teach. Principals and assistant principals could teach a class in their school or could work with a teacher to team-teach a class. Central office administrators could substitute teach one day every month or two. Citizens who seek to impact education or who are vocal in their thoughts about schools could substitute teach.

The benefits are endless. Being reminded of the demands and the joys of teaching could be a good reality check. Conversations between teachers, administrators and citizens could now have a common or shared base of information. Morale could benefit as teachers see people who are typically away from classrooms coming into classrooms and sharing the teachers' experience.

Some retail companies and some restaurants require upper management to get out of their offices and go work in the stores to be face to face with customers and to be face to face with employees who are on the front lines. Schools could benefit from a similar plan. Is there any real reason to not do this?

SCHOOL THOUGHT 36

What thoughts go through the minds of students, teachers, principals, school secretaries, school cafeteria workers, school custodians, bus drivers and all other education workers each morning before school? Does everyone hope for a great day of learning? Do some people work with heroic determination while other people barely go through the motions of their tasks?

Now, contrast that with the thoughts of all people involved with a high school marching band as those people move from the end of the school day to the start of a long, demanding marching band practice. Isn't it likely that there is a stronger sense of anticipation, commitment and effort from the marching band participants for band practice than there was from the total school community for the overall day at school?

What can be learned from and borrowed from marching band success that could be helpful to school success in general? The same question could emerge from success experienced by students in school clubs, theatrical presentations, athletic teams and chorus concerts. The answer is varied, but two parts of the answer are (1) being noticed and (2) being rewarded. Notice comes in many forms, including comments to students during class—"Great answer," "Exactly right," "Close, very close. Let's take that answer and build on it." Letters or phone calls to parents and guardians of students telling about good or great work the student did can be effective. Rewards should come in forms such as banquets and trophies for academic achievement, that are more elaborate than any other celebration at school and in the form of more school ceremonies going to scholars than to athletes. Do we give rings to straight-A students just as we do to state champion sports teams?

When children are very young, they often say to adults, "watch me" as they run, ride a bicycle, kick a ball or play on a swing set. Older children and teenagers may no longer say the words "watch me," but they still yearn for adults to notice them and to reward their efforts. Adults who watched and cheered for children who rode a bicycle taught those children to thrive on being noticed, acknowledged and rewarded. Continuing to notice, acknowledge and reward that same bicycle rider as he or she goes from child to teenager can bring wonderful results.

SCHOOL THOUGHT 37

"You hate school, don't you?"

"Yes, sir," the 15-year-old said with more enthusiasm than he had shown in the preceding 10-minute investigation of his misbehavior. "I come only because the law makes me."

"Well, is there any class at school that you like and do well in?"

"Yeah, gym." The student was visibly excited by the thought of gym class.

The principal asked, "What's your favorite part of gym class?"

"Basketball. I really like basketball."

"OK. Let's go to the gym." The student and the principal went from the office to the gym. The student obeyed but had no idea of what to expect.

The principal handed him a basketball. "You told me you hate math. You said that fractions are weird. True, they are, but let's make sense out of them. If you shoot 10 free throws, how many will go in?"

The student thought deeply and said with some confidence, "I guess five."

"OK. You shoot 10 free throws and I'll keep track of the results."

"Zero out of one. One out of two. One out of three. One out of four. Two out of five. Two out of six. Three out of seven. Four out of eight. Five out of nine. Five out of ten. Way to go."

The student smiled and said, "I can do better."

The principal said, "I agree. You can do better in basketball and in school. Here's the deal. As long as you do not get sent to the office again, you and I will begin each day with 10 free throws while everyone else is in homeroom. By the way, you made five out of 10, what fraction is that?"

"I guess it's five-tenths."

"Right!"

The student was never sent to the office again. Fractions now had a purpose and a connection to real life. He set a new goal of eight out of 10 and reached it. He even began converting the fractions to percentages.

True story. Extreme teaching meets creative discipline. Everyone involved won. The principal often told students, "If you take me on, I'll win. If you cooperate with me, we'll both win."

SCHOOL THOUGHT 38

Students memorize the words to popular songs and the scripts of clever commercials. What would happen if schools advertised being S.M.A.R.T. to convince students that success at school is important?

"Be S.M.A.R.T. That means be Successful, Motivated, Ambitious, Responsible and Tenacious. S.M.A.R.T. is not what you were born with. S.M.A.R.T. is what you become when you use your ability fully, when you work seriously and when you settle for nothing less than your absolute best. Everyone can be S.M.A.R.T. Everyone can be Successful, Motivated, Ambitious, Responsible and Tenacious. So, study, then study more and after that study some more. Think. Listen. Participate in class discussions. Ask questions. Complete all homework on time and done correctly. Be S.M.A.R.T."

Advertising works. It may be an extreme idea, but imagine what could happen if advertising did for success at school what it does for soft drinks and fast food.

SCHOOL THOUGHT 39

Schools without many interior walls were being built in many parts of the country in about 1970 or so. The idea was to create large, open areas in which multiple classes could work. Through this communal openness, it was hoped, creative and dynamic learning experiences would flourish. The eventual result was costly renovations to install the walls for separate classrooms that should have always been there.

Beware of educational fads, superficial ideas, trendy social engineering schemes and other desperately grasped quick-fix illusions. School almost always boils down to what happens in the classroom between teacher, students, ideas and activities. Architecture that enhances education is appreciated, but the building does not teach. Old, dysfunctional buildings may interfere with a great school climate, but renovation of the building alone will not cause instant and lasting improvement in student achievement.

The purpose of a school is to cause learning. We must do that which most effectively and most efficiently causes learning. All else we reject, even the hottest fads embraced by corporate Americans or famous psychologists. A magnificent obsession with causing learning can help guide decisions about curriculum, instructional materials, teaching methods and budgets. Keep all decisions rigidly consistent with and supportive of the purpose, which is to cause learning.

SCHOOL THOUGHT 40

"The students are so apathetic. Nobody does homework. I'm sick of it." The teacher really was frustrated and weary.

The principal listened to the rest of the story and then asked, "Is anyone in your classes doing the homework consistently?"

The teacher replied, "Sure. Maybe half or more in each class, but some never do it."

"OK. Next week, tell the students who turn in each daily assignment that you will give me good news about them and I'll reward them."

In three weeks, completion of homework increased from about 60 percent to about 80 percent. That is not perfect, but it is progress. There is more good news in schools than is sometimes noticed; celebrate the good news. The students appreciate the recognition, and the adults enjoy the opportunity to realize that some good work is being done. Problems happen and they must be resolved, but most students at most schools do what they are supposed to do most of the time. Sure, "most" needs to move up to "almost all" and then to "all," but celebrate the small victories along the way. The goal is for every student to learn. As more students learn more, celebrate the steps that lead to all students learning all.

SCHOOL THOUGHT 41

When a school scores 72 on a test that last year it scored a 68 on, did every student at the school improve? Probably not. The score may suggest that generally, throughout the school, enough students made enough improvement that the overall score increased by four points. Still, the score of 72 tells nothing about individual students. Schools educate individual students; schools graduate individual students; teachers grade work done by individual students.

When the economy grows at a 2.6 percent rate versus a 2.4 percent rate in an earlier time period, did every business grow as part of the 0.2 percentage point increase? No. Some companies thrived, some grew a little, others maintained, some decreased and a few went broke.

So, schools cannot be content with overall numbers that permit great achievement by some students to mask low results from other students. Those people who evaluate schools using one comprehensive number should beware of the distortion such measurements may include.

Is Jennifer learning? Is Shawn learning? Results for each individual student, those real people who come to school, are more important than any composite score.

SCHOOL THOUGHT 42

Remember that mild-mannered, very experienced legendary teacher who seemed to have taught every student's grandparents and parents? The teacher was of average physical size but dominated the classroom with the aura of competence. She cared deeply about students. She relentlessly assigned work that she insisted would be done on time, correctly and completely. It was. How did that teacher succeed so well in the days before learning style research, brain-based research, multiple intelligences, differentiated instruction, cultural competence, education reform and high-stakes testing?

That teacher challenged, cared, interacted, made learning interesting, made learning matter, connected learning to real life right now, knew the subject expertly, insisted on results, measured individual student achievement, exemplified a life of learning and applied acting techniques to command the rapt attention of the class. It still works.

SCHOOL THOUGHT 43

Even the best teacher, the most prepared teacher, the most competent teacher, the most energetic teacher, the most interactive teacher can have an absolutely terrible day at school. Then what?

The severe pessimist would quit. The incurable optimist would overlook the trouble and expect a better tomorrow. The realist would evaluate what went wrong, determine which of those factors are within the teacher's control, make some reasonable adjustments and persist through a hoped-for, planned-for, prepared-for day: tomorrow.

Still, terrible days do occur, and those days can discourage, frustrate, exhaust and disappoint the most determined teacher. That's when you buy your favorite ice cream, rent your favorite movie, take your favorite walk, listen to your favorite music, read your favorite inspirational words or take a long, deep, rich gaze into the night sky to remember the endless wonder of the human adventure. Then you try again tomorrow.

Take care of yourself. Teaching can be a blessing and a joy. Teaching can be heartbreaking and headache causing. Be good to you so you can be great to students.

SCHOOL THOUGHT 44

Human beings appear to have an inherent, innate, natural drive to learn, will to learn, urge to learn. Infants are fascinated by all that surrounds them. Children eagerly seek to learn what a big brother or a big sister knows. Middle school students seek to match or exceed the skills of high school students: "When we get to high school, we'll really show them."

Is it possible that school itself—the routine procedures, the predictable worksheets, the generic textbooks, the daily grind—saps the inherent curiosity, urge to learn, drive to know and will to become an expert in that which fascinates a student?

Is it possible that school itself—the routine procedures, the predictable meetings, the generic professional development workshops, the generic paperwork, the daily grind—saps the original commitment, urge to teach, drive to excel and will to become a scholar that was once burning within teachers?

Think of what you always hoped classes would be when you daydreamed as a student. Think of what you promised yourself you would do when you got to be a teacher. Live the daydream. Keep the promise. Slay the ordinary, the dull, the lifeless, generic, bureaucratic void that too often passes for school. Lead the quiet revolution against the ordinary with one fascinating moment after another fascinating moment in your classroom. Live your original daydream. Keep your original promise. Be the teacher you were born to be.

SCHOOL THOUGHT 45

The drama, the essence, the meaning, the ultimate, the truth, the best of life is interpersonal.

Computer software really does create a nearly convincing simulation of fascination, entertainment, excitement, exploration and wonder, but it is all virtual. It's all person to computer screen, not person to person.

Technology offers educators a valuable array of new instructional devices and new instructional opportunities. Use them for all they are worth, but remember that even at its best, technology cannot match the face-to-face, brain-to-brain, idea-to-idea, intrigue-to-intrigue, curiosity-to-curiosity, fascination-to-fascination, question-to-question, answer-to-answer impact of interactive teaching and interactive learning between two or more real people who are living real lives of real thinking and of real learning right now.

SCHOOL THOUGHT 46

As late summer changed to early autumn, a teacher found that her students' original level of interest in school when the new school year began had more than declined. It had changed into intentional, continuous refusal to cooperate. Despite every traditional, modern, creative or recommended teaching method used, most of the students were defiant. Despite all disciplinary actions used, most of the students were defiant.

The crisp, clear, clean autumn air on a particularly lovely October day took the teacher's attention from classroom frustration to nature's beauty. This gave her an idea. She compiled some information about Earth's axis, Earth's daily rotation, Earth's annual orbit around the Sun, the Moon's monthly orbit around Earth and how these factors and others impact or do not impact the changing seasons.

The students had endless questions. "Can astronauts go to the Sun?" "Is it summer all the time in Florida?" "I like winter best. Why can't we have more winter?" "Why don't you feel upside down at the South Pole?" "Sometimes it gets warm in winter. How can that happen?" "I heard that seasons change because Earth tilts, but we're so far from the Sun, why does that matter?" "How long does it take to go to the Moon?" "Is it true that an astronaut hit a golf ball on the Moon?" "Why does the shape of the Moon change?" "What's an eclipse? Does the Sun really go away?"

From those questions came discussions, reports, activities, projects, interdisciplinary units, amazing learning, unprecedented cooperation and superior behavior. For the rest of the school year, the same process continued with other topics of interest. Everyone lived and learned happily ever after.

SCHOOL THOUGHT 47

A student asked, "We already did that work on fractions. Why are we doing fractions again?"

The teacher replied, "You're exactly right. Good thinking. As Shawn just said, we are doing fractions. Great introduction to our topic today, Shawn. You get five bonus points. Let's start with Shawn telling us everything he can remember about fractions. Ready, Shawn? Go."

Shawn did not know what had just happened, but he knew that he had just received five bonus points, he knew that the teacher had complimented him and he knew he was on center stage. He responded with a long list of fraction facts and fraction uses and fraction ideas. This is a different result than if the teacher had said, "Shawn, quit complaining. We have to cover this material. Just do what you're told."

SCHOOL THOUGHT 48

Pick your battles. A principal once asked a colleague, "We can see the direction this decision is headed. Do we fight it or not?"

The colleague replied, "I would fight it in a limited way. No ground troops."

The principal completed the thought. "But heavy bombing. Good idea."

The bombs were sent in the form of e-mail. Those messages dropped some new information to people who were concerned about the content of the emerging decision and who were concerned about the process a small but vocal interest group was using.

The result was that the decision was delayed for one year until all groups potentially impacted by the decision could be represented on a committee that would report findings and recommendations.

Pick your battles. It is useful to win battles, but it is necessary to win wars. It can be wise to occasionally concede a temporary battle to concentrate on winning an enduring war. Pick your battles, and pick your tactics wisely.

SCHOOL THOUGHT 49

It is worth it. Teaching is worth it. Teaching is worth the extra hours for bus duty or game duty or hallway duty. Teaching is worth the frustration of attending long meetings that accomplish nothing. Teaching is worth the frustration of hearing school board members or state and national political leaders discuss the big, broad, generalizations that "no student will be left behind," yet knowing that those same people have never worked in a school for one day in a direct effort to avoid keeping any student from being left behind. Teaching is worth long nights of grading papers and weekends that seem short due to more time spent grading papers. Teaching is worth it because students are worth it and because learning is worth it.

There are two disclaimers: (1) If you are cut out for teaching, if you have the heart, mind and soul of a teacher, no other job will satisfy you; however, if you are not cut out for teaching, you will likely impose misery on yourself, your students and your colleagues. In that case, it is wise to find a better job match. (2) If circumstances out of your control—physical health, mental health, family problems, death of a loved one, career burnout or other factors—make it impossible for you to teach well, consider a leave of absence or a transfer to a different school or a transfer to a nonteaching job in the school district. Perhaps with the passage of time in a new setting you can recharge your battery, renew your mind, restore your convictions and energize your commitment to teaching. Seek wise advice and counsel.

SCHOOL THOUGHT 50

"I feel so isolated, all day, every day, I rarely see another adult for more than a minute or two. We're always in such a hurry. I love being with the students, but it would be great to have some conversation with adults, too."

Some teachers cherish the entrepreneurial aspect of being the sole proprietor of their classroom. The classroom becomes a place where the teacher and the students creatively invent, explore, discover, think, analyze, learn and succeed.

Some teachers resent the isolation from other adults that teaching can foster. Everyone goes into their classrooms, and from the start of the school day to the end of the typically busy school day, there is little opportunity for meaningful interaction. Some faculties plan Friday after-school visits at a local coffee shop. Some faculties plan monthly potluck dinners at school or at a community center. Some faculties create occasional times during the school day for students to be in an assembly with volunteers—including central office personnel and community members—to supervise students while teachers meet.

Be aware of the tendency to be or to feel isolated, and make time for the adults at school to interact.

SCHOOL THOUGHT 51

Success equals removing the causes of failure or the excuses for failure. There are simple actions that can be taken to counter each of the following explanations for failure:

"I don't have a pencil."
"I don't have any paper."
"I lost my copy of the homework."
"I forgot."
"I left it at home."
"I thought it was due tomorrow."
"I didn't understand how to do that."

One teacher became annoyed with students who, on a test, always answered the short, objective questions—such as "Who wrote the Declaration of Independence"—but who did no work on longer questions such as "Write a 30-second radio commercial giving three reasons for or against a current presidential candidate."

The teacher changed the format of the long questions. Instead of presenting the question and then leaving lots of space for an answer, the teacher organized the structure of the answer.

Here's an example. "Write three paragraphs with three sentences each telling why schools should continue to have sports and other extracurricular activities, even when budgets for schools have to be cut."

First paragraph:

- Sentence one:
- Sentence two:
- Sentence three:

The same format continued for the second and third paragraphs. The result was that almost every student completed the essay question. The only difference was that the teacher helped the students divide the long task into short, easily done tasks. Students could see how to structure and organize their long answers, so they wrote what they knew rather than skipping the question for any excuse from "It's too long" to "How do I get started?"

Sometimes a simple format change to show students how to organize ideas is all it takes to release an endless expression of thinking.

SCHOOL THOUGHT 52

"That wasn't us. That was the other class. We were good. The other class caused all of those problems for the substitute teacher."

The teacher was not convinced, but he agreed to call the substitute teacher to double-check. The truth was that a mistake had been made. It was an honest mistake: the teacher works closely with a few other teachers to vary the daily schedule. They use a modified block schedule, with teachers having groups of students for class sessions of longer amounts of time, but on fewer days. The substitute teacher had been confused by this schedule and had misidentified the groups of students in his report.

The teacher explained the confusion to the students, whose claim of innocence had been accurate. The teacher also distributed cookies to the students. "Hey, we'll take cookies for mistakes anytime," they smiled. Everything was resolved. The teacher got accurate information. The teacher also corrected the mistake and made it up to the students.

The other class, which really had misbehaved, received the well-known, predictable, automatic penalty used in that school for misbehavior with a substitute teacher. Justice was done. Cooperation was rewarded, and misbehavior was punished.

SCHOOL THOUGHT 53

Some jobs, some work, some careers can be put into very specific, precise, procedural and predictable formulas. The daily tasks are by the book with no variation, innovation or adventure. Here's how it is done, do it this way every time, every day, every year. Don't change anything.

Teaching that really causes learning cannot be reduced to a prefabricated activity or a sterile formula of learning equals read the chapter plus do the vocabulary work plus write the report plus watch the video plus review notes the night before the test: that may sound appealing, but it will not work with the certainty that a formula suggests is available.

Even the idea of connecting what students know, are interested in and/or are good at with new knowledge to be gained involves creativity, openness to concepts, varied activities, multiple resources and bold academic ventures that no formula can contain. Extreme Teaching presents a concept and a map, but there are many Extreme Teaching routes on the map that will take a teacher and students from what is known to what needs to be known.

Real teaching includes a potential for dynamic human interaction that transcends the limits of any formula, interaction that truly creates unique, new, unprecedented learning experiences that connect the unique knowledge, interests and talents of one unique classroom of students with the new knowledge, interests and talents to be acquired in the current class. Wow! Making all of those connections is to teaching, learning and school what the idea of traveling to other planets is for astronauts—an outlook on learning, an outlook on life that has no limits on what can be thought and that has no limits on what can be pursued.

SCHOOL THOUGHT 54

The question is not how math can be taught better. The question is not how science or language arts, social studies or international languages, health or computer applications, band or chorus can be taught better.

The question is how teachers can cause the learning of math by students. The goal is for students to learn math. The action taken to cause learning is teaching. How can the students, the teacher and math interact with each other so math is mastered by the students? Try this: begin with the result that every student learned math, and then work backwards to identify each step that helped cause the learning, then implement those steps from start to finish.

SCHOOL THOUGHT 55

Adults often say about teenagers, "They think they know everything and adults know nothing." True, the teenage years are often a time when 13-year-olds or 19-year-olds or everyone in between those ages has compiled a combined level of confidence, competence, physical health and academic progress to feel quite capable of making decisions and of rejecting advice.

Well, the adults still are in charge, and teenagers need to stay within proper guidelines, rules and behaviors. Still, the teenager's confidence that he or she knows everything can become a teaching resource. Use what teenagers do know, help them identify what they do not know and create connections between those two bodies of knowledge. Teenagers may give themselves more credit than they deserve, but it would be unfortunate to give teenagers less credit than they deserve.

Be glad that teenagers "think they know it all." That confirms a great goal—to know it all. Now lead them toward that total knowledge goal by gently but clearly showing them what they do not yet know. Then show them how what they really know can get them—with lots of work—to full knowledge.

SCHOOL THOUGHT 56

If you could travel in time, what year and what place would be your destination?

One teacher answered this way: "I would travel through time to high school football practice in 1971. I would practice relentlessly to prevent the many years since then of wishing that I had tried harder back then when I was given a chance."

Do students realize the powerful yet fleeting possibility of the current moment and the current opportunities at school? When teachers can convince students of the importance of making the most of each moment, a great service will be done. The present moment can become more productive! The future can have less regret.

SCHOOL THOUGHT 57

I am responsible for my actions.

If other people act silly, I can still behave correctly.

If other people cheat, I can still be honest.

If other people goof off, I can still pay attention.

If other students never turn in work, I can still turn in my work on time, done completely, done correctly, always.

If other students try to start fights, I can still get along with people and I can avoid fighting.

If other students disrupt a class, I can still control myself, behave properly and cooperate with the teacher.

If other people lie, I can still tell the truth.

I am responsible for my actions.

If other people waste their time, I can still use my time well.

If other people try to see what misbehavior or crimes they can get away with, I can still see what good work I can accomplish.

If other students steal, I can still respect the property of another person and leave it alone.

If other students make silly or mean comments, I can ignore those people and their comments.

If other students make a mistake toward me, I may want to get revenge, but that means those people are playing me for a fool. No matter what other people do or say, I can still be in control of what I do and of what I say.

If other students gossip or meddle, I can still remain silent. It is OK sometimes to say nothing.

I am responsible for my actions.

If other people are lazy, I can work.

If other people curse and talk trash, I do not have to do that. I can speak properly, or I can be quiet.

If other people smoke tobacco, drink alcohol or use drugs, I can keep myself tobacco-free, alcohol-free and drug-free.

If other people make excuses and blame everyone else for their problems or for their mistakes, I can still take responsibility and make myself get results.

I am responsible for getting proper results in my life. I do not allow myself to make excuses.

I cannot control what happens around me, what other people do or what other people say. I can control my reactions, and I am responsible for my reactions. Sometimes, it is best to do nothing or to say nothing. When it is right to act or to speak, I am responsible for what I do and for what I say.

If other people take the easy way out and give up, I can still take charge and find a way to complete my duties.

No matter what anyone else says or does or thinks, I have been taught right from wrong and I have been taught good from bad. I know right from wrong, good from bad.

I am responsible for my actions.

SCHOOL THOUGHT 58

"That's the answer to a question we'll get to in just a minute. Good thinking. Hold onto that idea. I'll get right back to you."

The question asked was "Who won the presidential election in the year 2000?" The student's answer was "Bill Clinton." The teacher very favorably acknowledged the answer. She will make sure all the students know that George W. Bush won the 2000 election; however, she did not totally reject the student's answer because there are uses for that answer and because the goal is to cause learning. What is gained by saying "Wrong!" to the student? The student might give up, misbehave, quit or withdraw into silence.

The teacher did communicate "wrong" in a very creative way, which kept the students eagerly awaiting how and when the teacher would return to the answer of "Bill Clinton."

SCHOOL THOUGHT 59

Do students benefit from having stories read out loud to them? The stories could be anything from childhood favorites to Greek myths, from biography to the newspaper's front-page lead article.

The answer can be yes, even for middle school or high school students. The teacher reads a story out loud, stopping occasionally and having the students determine what the next word in the story will _____. See, you read that and inserted the word *be* in the blank. As a reader, you had to read and to think a bit differently than if the word *be* had been put there for you. Similar thinking can occur in classrooms when students have to anticipate and identify missing words from stories read aloud.

SCHOOL THOUGHT 60

The process of electing a president of the United States is a topic that many students know enough about for a teacher to build on so connections can be made with what is known and what needs to be known. School thoughts 61–66 show one sequence of teaching activities that were designed to make those connections to cause new learning—in this example to the electoral college process.

The sequence begins with a discussion of five questions that help the teacher identify what is known. That process continues with some introductory vocabulary terms.

Students then consider how score is kept in high school basketball games, followed by a new scoring system that functions as the electoral college in a presidential elections. Some more precise and directed work with the electoral college follows. The electoral college really is a confusing process that many adults misunderstand, so it takes some work, but actually doing the math of electoral votes helps.

The teacher then gives a short writing task not for a grade, but to show himself what the students understood and do not yet understand. Based on the results of that task, the teacher creates a story to help students better learn about the election process.

To recap, the initial knowledge of students about elections and then about basketball are used to create connections with the presidential election process. Electoral votes are then counted. A reality check shows the teacher what is understood and what is misunderstood. A story is created to make new connections between what is known, what is becoming known, what is becoming known partially and what is not yet known at all. The result is that students learn about the presidential election process and see it with a new perspective.

SCHOOL THOUGHT 61

Presidential election 2000:

1. What big, national election was held in November 2000?
2. What do you remember about that election?
3. How was the winner of that election determined?
4. Who participated in determining the winner of that election?
5. What was unusual about the results of that election? Did the winner really win? On what basis did the losing candidate have some claim to victory? Or did he have any claim to victory?

Vocabulary:

- George W. Bush
- Dick Cheney
- Al Gore
- Joe Lieberman
- popular vote
- U.S. Congress
- electoral vote
- Democrat and Republican
- debate
- paid political advertisement
- campaign
- election

1. _____ Give speeches, shake hands, advertise and seek to convince voters.
2. _____ When two or more candidates appear together to present their ideas about issues and to show the differences between their ideas.
3. _____ The Republican candidate for president; was governor of Texas; during 1989–1993, his father was president.

4. _____ The Democrat candidate for president; he has been the vice president of the United States and before that was a U.S. senator from Tennessee, just as his father had been.

5. _____ The votes of the people, one at a time, voting in their neighborhoods.

6. _____ The votes of the states—if a candidate gets the most popular votes in a state, that candidate gets all of these votes from the state.

7. _____ The two major political parties in the United States.

8. _____ The Democratic candidate for vice president; he has been the U.S. Senator from Connecticut.

9. _____ The Republican candidate for vice president; he used to be Secretary of Defense and before that was a U.S. Representative from Wyoming.

10. _____ An example of this would be a television commercial or a radio commercial that the candidate and his or her supporters paid for.

SCHOOL THOUGHT 62

	1st Quarter	2nd Quarter	3rd Quarter	4th Quarter	Final Score
Team A	12	14	12	16	54
Team B	8	8	13	20	49

- Which team won this basketball game?
- Which team was ahead at halftime?

Now, change the scoring system to use the electoral college method. Each successive quarter becomes more important and is worth more electoral points/votes.

	1st Quarter	2nd Quarter	3rd Quarter	4th Quarter	Final Score
Team A	1	2	0	0	3
Team B	0	0	3	4	7

- Which team won the game with this counting system?
- Which team was ahead at halftime with this counting system?

What is similar about the two scoring systems?

What is different about the two scoring systems?

Is one system more fair? More accurate? Based on what?

SCHOOL THOUGHT 63

Electoral votes—ancient accident waiting to happen again or honorable, noble system continuing the wisdom of the nation's founders?

FACT: There are 538 electoral votes because $435 + 100 + 3 = 538$

WAIT: Where did we get the 435? _____

And the 100? _____

And the 3? _____

OK. So, if you need a majority of the 538, you would need 270 to win, because 269–269 would be a tie and that would get really complicated. It can happen and it can be resolved, but it is complicated.

Here's the really weird part of the electoral vote process. If you get more popular votes—the votes of the people—in a state, you get ALL of the electoral votes from that state. For example, if the popular vote is 745,501 to 745,001, the candidate who won the popular votes by 500 gets ALL of the electoral votes from that state—for example, 11 electoral votes to 0.

So, if a candidate for president wins the biggest states in the nation, that candidate gets elected president even without winning any other state. Here's how:

California:	54	New York:	33	Texas:	32	Florida:	25
Pennsylvania:	23	Illinois:	22	Ohio:	21	Michigan:	18
New Jersey:	15	N. Carolina:	14	Virginia:	13		

How close was the electoral vote in November 2000?

Gore: _____ electoral votes
Bush: _____ electoral votes
Total: 538

SCHOOL THOUGHT 64

If you know which states were "won" by which candidate in popular votes, you can determine how many total electoral votes each candidate got.

Please use the list on this page and information from the almanac or websites to get the popular vote and the electoral vote totals for Mr. Bush and for Mr. Gore.

State	Bush: Popular Vote	Bush: Electoral Vote	Gore: Popular Vote	Gore: Electoral Vote
Alabama				
Alaska				
Arizona				
Arkansas				
California				
Colorado				
Connecticut				
Delaware				
District of Columbia				
Florida				
Georgia				
Hawaii				
Idaho				
Illinois				
Indiana				
Iowa				
Kansas				
Kentucky				

continued

State	Bush: Popular Vote	Electoral Vote	Gore: Popular Vote	Electoral Vote
Louisiana	_____	_____	_____	_____
Maine	_____	_____	_____	_____
Maryland	_____	_____	_____	_____
Massachusetts	_____	_____	_____	_____
Michigan	_____	_____	_____	_____
Minnesota	_____	_____	_____	_____
Mississippi	_____	_____	_____	_____
Missouri	_____	_____	_____	_____
Montana	_____	_____	_____	_____
Nebraska	_____	_____	_____	_____
Nevada	_____	_____	_____	_____
New Hampshire	_____	_____	_____	_____
New Jersey	_____	_____	_____	_____
New Mexico	_____	_____	_____	_____
New York	_____	_____	_____	_____
North Carolina	_____	_____	_____	_____
North Dakota	_____	_____	_____	_____
Ohio	_____	_____	_____	_____
Oklahoma	_____	_____	_____	_____
Oregon	_____	_____	_____	_____
Pennsylvania	_____	_____	_____	_____
Rhode Island	_____	_____	_____	_____
South Carolina	_____	_____	_____	_____
South Dakota	_____	_____	_____	_____
Tennessee	_____	_____	_____	_____
Texas	_____	_____	_____	_____
Utah	_____	_____	_____	_____
Vermont	_____	_____	_____	_____
Virginia	_____	_____	_____	_____
Washington	_____	_____	_____	_____
West Virginia	_____	_____	_____	_____

continued

State	Bush: Popular Vote	Electoral Vote	Gore: Popular Vote	Electoral Vote
Wisconsin	_____	_____	_____	_____
Wyoming	_____	_____	_____	_____
Totals:	_____	_____	_____	_____

Why does Al Gore wish he had been able to campaign just a little more in New Hampshire where the popular vote was 48 percent Bush, 47 percent Gore?

SCHOOL THOUGHT 65

Use each of the following words or terms at least once—campaign, popular, electoral, 538, 270 and states—in a two- or three-sentence response to the question below. Underline the required words or terms when you use them.

Explain how the president of the United States is elected.

SCHOOL THOUGHT 66

Once upon a time (actually it was in the year 1789) a new constitution for a fairly new country was established. Most of the people who lived in this country were involved in farming. There were some cities, some towns and some villages, but many people lived in wide-open spaces even if they were in a community. There were 13 states in this country, which was called the _____.

The states of this country had debated and approved a new constitution during 1787–1789. One part of this new constitution explained how a _____ of the United States would be elected. The year 1789 was way before television, radio, the Internet or other electronic communication. In 1789 there were no airplanes, trains or cars. All of this meant that the entire country could not participate very easily in a _____ and in an election for president of the United States.

There was an idea presented: The people in each state could choose a group of people whom they knew and trusted to represent them, who would travel to Washington, D.C., to help select the president. These people were called electors and they would cast _____. It became common for the electors from each state to associate with a presidential candidate. This meant that when a particular candidate for president won the popular vote in a state, his or her electors would be the people who went to Washington, D.C., and those electors would cast all of their electoral votes for their associated candidate. Each state has a number of electoral votes equal to the number of people who are from that state in the United States _____ and in the United States House of _____.

Even though we had modern communication methods and modern transportation methods in year 2000, we still used the system of popular votes and electoral votes. Some people think we should just add up all of the popular votes, but that change has not been made.

(Use some of the words below for the blanks above.)

Canada	Real votes	Electoral votes
England	Popular votes	Government
United States of America	Individual votes	Senate
Governor	Court	President
Commons	Representatives	Campaign

SCHOOL THOUGHT 67

Try starting class with this statement to see if students' interest and enthusiasm can be inspired: "Raise your hand if you like pizza." Most, if not all, students know something about baseball, pizza and/or television. The chart below shows how to easily organize some initial instructional thought starter ideas to make connections with these. What classroom activities could show connections between (1) momentum, inertia and baseball; (2) nutrition, pizza, and the impact of heat on food and (3) electricity, technology and television? Write those activities in the third column below and then create full lesson plans from those thought starters.

Knowledge students need to master in science class	Topic or teaching method used to make connections	Classroom activity used to cause learning
Momentum Inertia	Baseball	1. 2.
The impact of heat on food Nutrition	Pizza	1. 2.
Electricity Technology	Television	1. 2.

SCHOOL THOUGHT 68

Education reforms come and education reforms go. Then more education reforms come and those education reforms go. The history of education in the United States includes a persistent willingness to try something new. Trying something new that is better could be helpful if it is implemented well. But trying something new only because it is new wastes time, money and work and erodes people's willingness to try more new approaches.

Three constants have endured all education reforms: teachers, students and a curriculum. Certainly what teachers do and how they do it, what students do and how they do it and what the curriculum includes and excludes change over time; however, where there is a school, even with long-distance Internet learning, the process involves teachers, students and a curriculum.

The enduring presence of teachers, students and curriculum suggests that those three elements of education are essential. What education reform does that truly impacts favorably the work of students and teachers with a curriculum could be significant. Reform that does not benefit students, teachers and curriculum is of questionable worth.

SCHOOL THOUGHT 69

Violence at school is tragic beyond measure. The very possibility that a student would kill students or adults at school is a horrible, yet realistic, part of today's school setting.

Many actions can be taken to prevent, minimize or resolve school violence, including: (1) law enforcement officers in schools, (2) metal detectors and security surveillance cameras throughout schools, (3) joint actions, ventures and facilities shared by the juvenile justice system and the school system and (4) more alternative schools that work with violent offenders so that the large majority of students who do cooperate can go to school without a criminal in their midst.

There is another idea to consider: students do not destroy places where they are taken seriously and where they are fascinated. School violence is not matched by violent teenage crimes in shopping malls, amusement parks or swimming pools, although the same age group and the same people go to those places. There could be something about school that causes it to be a place where so many teenage murderers have acted out their crimes. Making school real, making school matter, making school fascinating can enhance academic results by students while also creating a mutual commitment between school and students. That commitment could result in safer schools, because children and teenagers are less likely to be violent at places they value.

SCHOOL THOUGHT 70

Technology can be used effectively by teachers and by students; however, technology does not need to be included in a lesson plan just because a teacher has not used a computer with the students for three days. Use technology when its use is the best way to cause learning. Make the technology work for you rather than making yourself work for the technology. Teachers need to lead computers, not follow them.

SCHOOL THOUGHT 71

Students can be impressed when they hear teachers talk about how much they—the teachers—love to learn, how much they love to read, how much they love to study, how much they eagerly seek new knowledge, new skills and new interests. Students sometimes think that adults stop learning when they complete high school, college or graduate school, and perhaps some adults do limit their learning efforts after they finish school. Teachers can and should keep learning. Teachers can and should show students they are continuing to learn. Teachers could even learn from a student who has knowledge, skills or interests a teacher does not have.

Teaching can be strengthened by setting the example that, as a teacher, you value continuation of your learning. Let the students see you learn. When students have a research paper to write, you could also do research and write a paper. When students are assigned a story to make up, write and present to the class, you could do the same assignment. There is power in leading by example. There is power in teaching and learning by example.

SCHOOL THOUGHT 72

School districts have policies. Teachers need to know the policies and need to follow the policies. "Well, I thought it would be OK." "You know, I never thought it would violate a policy." "I didn't bring up the subject, but the student asked me, so we had a discussion in class about it." "I guess there were forms to fill out and approval to get, but everyone is so busy, I just went on and arranged everything."

Follow the policies. If a policy needs to be changed, work to change the policy, but until a change is made, follow the current policy. Good intentions or lack of knowledge of the policy will not excuse policy violations by school district employees.

It is equally important to know the laws, usually state laws but occasionally federal laws, about education. Know the laws about schools, and follow those laws. Within policies and laws, teachers have much professional freedom, but stay within policies and laws.

SCHOOL THOUGHT 73

Great teachers are guaranteed to have opposition. Some students will complain that they are given too much work. Some parents or guardians will complain about the amount of homework, the teaching methods used, favoritism toward some students and other allegations. Colleagues may express resentment or jealousy.

"You're making all of us look bad," an experienced teacher said to the gentleman who was substitute teaching for a week.

The substitute replied with some confusion, "I'm just trying to do my job well. I didn't intend to cause a problem. What exactly did I do?"

The teacher bluntly answered. "You're all dressed up. We're pretty casual here."

The substitute had worn a typical suit that he wore to his advertising job on any given day. His week off from advertising to teach was actually a vacation he was giving himself. Imagine that—a person wanting to teach so much that he would take vacation time and then still get criticized for dressing too professionally.

Great teachers are guaranteed to have opposition. Teach greatly anyway. Be a great teacher anyway.

SCHOOL THOUGHT 74

Great teachers persist. The history of humankind is highlighted by honorable efforts that continued despite difficulties. The history of education includes countless stories from students whose lives changed because a teacher would not give up on a student and because a teacher would not let a student give up. Persistence ensures one or both of the following: (1) success or (2) the satisfaction of knowing that you did everything you possibly could do to make a difference. Persist. Persistence is an unsurpassed resource and power.

SCHOOL THOUGHT 75

Count the minutes so each minute will count. With two minutes left in a class it is easy to say, "Well, there's not much time to start anything else, so just pack up your books and get ready for the bell to ring."

Have a ready-made set of one-minute, two-minute, three-minute, four-minute and five-minute activities that are valid, productive uses of time. No basketball coach lets his or her players stop playing with two minutes left on the clock. No teacher should let time slip away, either.

Questions can be asked. Ideas can be discussed. Sentences can be written. Test questions can be practiced. A short video clip can be shown. A short story can be read aloud. Learning can be caused even in a short amount of time.

Thoreau was right: "As if you could kill time without injuring eternity."[1]

SCHOOL THOUGHT 76

Imagine the moment when all students in a classroom made an A on a test and fully understood the ideas, the material, the questions and the answers associated with their recent classroom work, studying, reading and test taking.

Now, imagine the sequence of actions the teacher created that led to this success by all students. Think of the action taken just before the students did so well on the test. Then think of the teacher's action just prior to that one. Keep going backward until you get to the starting point, when the teacher began working with the students on the ideas, material, questions and answers they would eventually master.

Sometimes it can be very insightful to analyze success by starting with the desired accomplishment and working backwards one step at a time to see what had to happen. Having identified the steps that led from success backward to step 1, you simply need to reverse the order, implement step 1 and continue sequentially until success is caused.

Note about school thoughts 77–86: These next 10 school thoughts add some details to school thought 69. School thoughts 77–86 combine to form an essay about school safety and school violence and are further encouragement for everyone associated with education to get real, to be realistic and to make school real—genuine, meaningful, useful, authentic, interesting, important, personal and fascinating.

Listen to some conversations students have and you will occasionally hear the words "for real." "For real, I really want to go to the game." "They broke up and it's for real." "Come on, you can sit with us," answered with "For real?" Those words can add emphasis, confirm agreement and just acknowledge reality. More students may take school more seriously and enthusiastically if they thought that school was for real.

SCHOOL THOUGHT 77

In the 1996 book *911: The School Administrator's Guide to Crisis Management*, the following reality check is provided:

> Consider school from a student's perspective. One seventh grader made the following comment to the author: "I was thinking about what would happen if one of these bullies brought a gun to school and shot me. I've just been thinking about that." That is a real comment from a 13-year-old in 1995. There is no record that he was hurt, harmed, threatened or challenged by other students. He makes reasonable grades and never gets in trouble. His concern is that another student might put a bullet through him. How can a 13-year-old concentrate on math and science when he genuinely feels that his life is threatened merely by attending school where some students are assumed to be prone to use violence at any moment?[2]

Many adults and students today are shocked by the tragic acts of school violence that continue to occur occasionally. Adults are likely to say, "That never happened when I was in school." We cannot turn the school clock back to a former era when violence in society was less common and when violence in school was rare. We cannot manage, staff and organize school now using the model, system, structure and perspective of the 1950s. We can only deal with the current reality. We can make schools safe, orderly and, consequently, more productive. How? Admit what the current reality is and begin dealing with it using all resources, technology, equipment, expertise and personnel available. The following ideas could be part of the total effort we can make.

No more studies on school violence are needed. We know the facts: School violence has increased, and anxiety about school violence is up. That does not mean that schools are out of control. Most students in most schools obey most rules most of the time. They are wonderful people to be with. The reality is that a very few students—but a larger number than in earlier decades—are committing criminal acts of violence at school. The increase in the number of students who are violent and the severity of their acts of violence make the current reality quite different from that of earlier decades.

SCHOOL THOUGHT 78

More alternative schools are needed. In addition to the increased number of violent students, the current reality also is that there are some disruptive students who are not violent but who are defiant, insubordinate and, thus far, incorrigible. The violent students and the repeatedly disruptive students need to be educated and reformed, but not necessarily at a typical school. It is unreasonable to expect one school staff and building to provide the perfect education for a range of students that goes from the habitual juvenile criminal to a future Harvard scholar. Some of the alternative schools needed now may be institutions of a type that has never before existed—such as a combination school/juvenile jail where offenders are placed by a joint decision of a court and a school district. Smaller school districts may need to combine resources and build these new institutions on a regional basis. These new alternative schools/institutions/facilities/jails could also be places where students who are suspended from school or who are expelled from a school district must report each day for school during their suspension or expulsion.

SCHOOL THOUGHT 79

Schools need to train school administrators and staff in emergency procedures. This training could borrow from the body of knowledge previously reserved for police officers, firefighters and other crisis management experts. This knowledge could help prevent, minimize or resolve incidents at schools.

SCHOOL THOUGHT 80

Schools need to increase the presence of school security officers. Perhaps we are at the point at which school security is needed in each high school and, possibly, in each middle school, in addition to being available to each elementary school. The presence of a law enforcement officer could help prevent much violence and many other misbehaviors at school. The law enforcement officer could also help investigate many discipline incidents currently taking up the time of school administrators, whose time could be better used on academic matters.

SCHOOL THOUGHT 81

We should be willing to use metal detectors and surveillance cameras at schools where these can be effective. What are we afraid of? For every reason (excuse?) about inconvenience or difficult logistics or budget limits, there are compelling reasons to use this technology—these devices could help reduce violence, help save lives and help build some increased sense of safety among students and educators. Actions to promote school safety may vary from school to school because needs and situations vary, but let's be willing to consider use of existing crime prevention equipment, technology and personnel.

SCHOOL THOUGHT 82

We as a society need to adjust our thinking about juvenile justice. The age of the offender is not the major factor; rather, the crime committed is the major factor. A 15-year-old accused of murder should be tried in court as an accused murderer, not as a juvenile accused of murder. Juveniles know how the juvenile justice system works, and they know that there are severe limits on what can be done to them. To some current juvenile offenders, crime seems to pay because the penalty is limited. Juvenile offenders would get the message if our society lessened consideration of age as a factor in deciding what penalty is given to a guilty person and increased consideration of the crime that was committed.

SCHOOL THOUGHT 83

We need to increase the communication and the collaboration between school districts and local courts. The juvenile offender who thinks that misbehavior at school is only going to result in some penalty imposed by the school administrators needs to know that there can be a simultaneous court hearing and, as warranted, a court action for serious misbehaviors at school. The mentality of some young people is that "If it happens at school it is not against the law, it is just against the school rule."

SCHOOL THOUGHT 84

We must staff schools to deal with the new realities. The principal of a school cannot manage every academic matter, every personnel matter, every question from every parent or guardian, every discipline matter, bus and cafeteria supervision, extracurricular supervision and the other routine matters of a school while also functioning as the constant security guard. We staff schools now the way we staffed schools 20, 30, 40, 50 or more years ago, despite the many changes and the increasing demands during those years. Would there be additional costs for additional staffing? Yes. As in much of life, we will get what we pay for. We can have safer and more secure schools if we are willing to do what is necessary and to invest resources wisely.

SCHOOL THOUGHT 85

Let's make school more meaningful for students. For too many students, school is boring, classes are dull and education seems to be unimportant. We can teach in ways that absolutely fascinate students and in ways that build their commitment to school. We can also reach out more effectively, perhaps using ideas such as the original concept of homeroom, which was designed to give teachers and students some time to communicate, to build trust, to know each other and to deal with issues or problems.

SCHOOL THOUGHT 86

We get more of what we reward. For the many students who do cooperate, who do behave well and who do their schoolwork, we can and we should acknowledge their efforts and achievements with rewards and recognition that surpass what schools and society reserve for athletes. Sure, athletes earn and deserve recognition, but if academic success and good behavior are our top priorities in school, let's give the top rewards and the most recognition for achievement in academics and in school citizenship.

Part of the challenge facing each community, each state and our nation on the subject of school violence is the tendency to confront this current issue with a 1950s model, structure and perspective about schools. To start dealing with the current problem of school violence, we must start with the current reality. There is good news: this is a problem we can deal with. There is more good news: most students are great people who are perfectly willing to follow school rules and to get along with people. The other students who are juvenile offenders need to be dealt with using unprecedented measures. The cooperative students need to be given the safest and best schools possible. If we get real we can get results. Safer and more secure schools are possible if we will do what is right, necessary, realistic, very practical and very feasible.

SCHOOL THOUGHT 87

The purpose of a school is to cause learning. What is the purpose of learning? To acquire wisdom. Wisdom is the extreme of learning. Wisdom results from potent, dynamic, continuous learning that probes the depths and the totality of knowledge, life, thinking, decision making, interaction and ethics. When schools cause learning that also includes learning how to learn, schools empower students to continue learning for a lifetime, to continue seeking wisdom and to continue acquiring wisdom.

What distinguishes learning from wisdom? To learn is to know; to be wise is to fully understand and to fully apply all proper learning. That is one more reason why it is vital for education to be real to students right now: so they can connect education with life right now and apply education to the real lives they are living right now. School can be more than preparation for life or experimentation with life or simulation of life. School can be taken seriously as real life right now if school gets real.

When school is real, students realize that learning is really important, and they are more likely to readily pursue wisdom. When school is not real, the urge to seek reality elsewhere increases and the interest in or commitment to school declines. From a student's perspective, if it is real, it is worth a commitment. Students will commit to something. Educators are convinced that students should commit to school. That is true, yet that commitment is not automatic.

The reality is that schools compete with many other possible uses of students' time, energy, minds, talents, interests and knowledge. School will not win that competition just because it is school and has the authoritative support of law. School will win that competition when it makes itself more beneficial to students than any other option students have for use of their time, energy, minds, talents, interests, knowledge, wants and needs.

SCHOOL THOUGHT 88

"I hate math." The student was sincere, but with the bluntness and the efficiency of student-speak he was more likely to use the short, shocking and, he hopes, sympathy-provoking "I hate math" than "I experience frustration and anxiety when an excessive amount of math is presented combined with a lingering memory of a math teacher years ago who made a mistake on my report card. I just harbor negative anticipatory thoughts when I enter math class."

A teacher could reply, "Yeah, I know what you mean. Math can get strange. Let's start by you writing down everything you already know about math. Numbers, adding, subtracting and all the rest." The student writes and the teacher responds.

"Perfect. You know a lot. What we are going to do next is based on what you already know. It's just the next step. It's like moving up from minor leagues to the major leagues. You're ready."

"I hate math" can be translated in many ways: "Math is hard." "I'm lazy." "I have too much homework." "My friend forgot my birthday." "I'm in a bad mood." The student whose teacher responds logically, "Oh, you're great in math" may enter an endless debate. The teacher who surprises the student with, "Yeah, I know what you mean" and then guides the student to realizing how much math he or she knows and can do already may swiftly reverse math hatred to math neutrality or acceptance, and then to math success.

SCHOOL THOUGHT 89

"Why do we have to keep studying English year after year? What's the big deal? We know how to talk and write."

What would happen if an English teacher used job applications, the driver's license study book and test, college applications, scholarship applications, essay contests sponsored by groups who pay cash to the student winners, television program scripts, print advertisements and e-mail messages as resources for a unit on practical applications of English skills?

What would happen if a local employer evaluated students' completed job applications and graded them not with letter grades such as A or F, but with grades of "would interview," "would not interview" or "would hire," "would not hire"? Perhaps English skills would become more real.

SCHOOL THOUGHT 90

"It's like when Watergate happened. The whole nation seemed to stand still waiting for that to end." The teacher spoke energetically to a class full of polite, capable students whose faces were blank. "You know, Watergate," the teacher continued.

The students did not know much about Watergate. The events of 1972–1974, which almost every person in the United States knew thoroughly then, are not events that current students have experienced. It is effective to update historical references so the events cited are within the lifetime of current students. If a teacher is working with 16-year-old students, then making references to events of the past five to ten years can increase the participation of students in the discussion and can make the discussion come alive much more.

SCHOOL THOUGHT 91

Here are some questions to reflect upon about classroom management, but first, consider this idea: great teaching is the best system of classroom management.

1. Think of the best teacher you ever had and what that teacher did to manage the classroom.
2. Think of the best idea you ever heard about classroom management.
3. How could theater training relate to classroom management?
4. How does the appearance of the classroom relate to classroom management?
5. How do lesson plans and instructional practices relate to classroom management? How does classroom time management also relate?
6. What is taking place when classroom management is great?
7. What is taking place when classroom mismanagement is occurring?

SCHOOL THOUGHT 92

Teacher: "Thomas, you need to put that paper away. We have all taken our books out, and we have turned to page 178. Today, we will continue learning about the ideas in the First Amendment to the United States Constitution. Who remembers one of the rights that is protected by the First Amendment?" The class discussion progresses well, and the teacher then explains that each student will write a letter to the editor of the school newspaper. The topic is: Our School's Dress Code: For or Against? The students are given some time right now in class to write their three-paragraph letters.

Teacher: Thomas, this is the second time I have told you to put that paper away. We are working on our letters to the editor. We are not reading that newspaper or magazine you brought. Now, give me the paper.

Thomas: I'm not giving this to anyone. It's not mine. I'll put it up. I already know what I'll write in my letter. I'll get it done right now.

You are the teacher; what do you do now with Thomas?

SCHOOL THOUGHT 93

Teacher: "OK, does everyone have the worksheet I just distributed? Good. The worksheet is due at the end of this period. You may use your book to find answers, but do your own work. Any questions? OK, please begin."

The teacher returns to his or her desk and begins grading some papers. The teacher glances up occasionally, and everything seems to be in order. There is no excessive noise and no movement in the classroom. Everyone seems to be working.

After about 10 minutes, the teacher gets up to walk around the room. Jennifer is sitting in the back of the room, and it is suddenly obvious that she has been writing notes to friends instead of writing answers to the questions on the worksheet.

Option A: "Jennifer, you are supposed to be working on the worksheet. This is no time to write notes. You really should not write notes in school. What do you have to say for yourself? Do you realize that the low grades you are getting in this class are because of misbehavior like this?"

Option B: The teacher walks over to Jennifer and holds out her hand. Jennifer does nothing. The teacher points to the notes Jennifer was writing. Jennifer still does nothing. The teacher grabs the notes, and Jennifer says, "My mother will hear about this." The teacher responds, "Yes, she certainly will." Other students are now watching Jennifer and the teacher.

Option C: The teacher walks to the door and says, "Jennifer, come here for a moment. I need to ask you a question. Please bring your worksheet with you." The teacher opens the door and steps out into the hallway with Jennifer, but the teacher can still see all of the students. "Jennifer, there is nothing on this sheet except what was printed by the publisher. You need to start working now."

What is good and what is bad about each option above: A, B and C?
Please write another possible way this situation could be resolved.
You are the teacher. What would you do?

SCHOOL THOUGHT 94

Discipline Referrals:

Scenario 1: John totally disrupted class today. He would not follow any instructions. I had to call him down several times, and he still would not follow my rules. He was just out of control. I had to put him in the hall, but he was just so loud there that the entire building could hear him, so I just sent him to the school's office.

Scenario 2: While we were discussing a science experiment about weather, John was out of his seat. I instructed him to sit, and eventually he did. While we continued the experiment, John decided to get up out of his seat again. I looked at him and I moved toward him. He got the message and sat down. In about two or three minutes, John was up again, and I told him to take a two-minute time out in the time out area of the room. He did this but did not follow all the time out rules about being completely quiet and still. After time out, John knocked a book off another student's desk, so I sent John to the team leader's room for a team time out. John took his books with him, and he was given the writing assignment about the experiment to do during team time out. After class, I checked on John and got his writing project from him, but he had done very little work. Since I had used classroom management methods and team methods, I brought John to the office to meet with a principal or with a counselor.

A. What are the differences in the content and the tone of the two referrals?
B. What could be the different perceptions of these two referrals by
the student's parent or guardian?
C. What could be better in a third version of a referral about this in-
cident?
D. What else could have been done to correct John's behavior?

SCHOOL THOUGHT 95

Great teachers speak selectively, knowing that not everything that comes into the brain should come out of your mouth. Why? Because your words and your actions cannot become the issue. When a student says, "You are unfair. I hate your class. I hate school," You do not say, "Well, school hates you, too." You edit your reply, you give yourself some think time and you return to the original issue—the fact that the student misbehaved. "Jason, you know right from wrong. You can follow instructions and you can do well at school. We need to deal with your misbehavior, get it resolved and then move on."

SCHOOL THOUGHT 96

Some tips and scenarios for practical communication:

- Do not reply quickly to a threat of "I'll go call my mother. She'll take care of you." Consider a sincere, neutral, "I would be glad to talk with your mother. That is a good idea."
- "After class" is the response to "May I go to the bathroom?"
- To "Well, she started it. She threw the pencil at me first," you might respond, "Don't let her mistake cause you to make a mistake. You didn't have to throw it back. If she threw it, she was wrong. But we also know for a fact that you threw it, and you were wrong to do that."
- "He called me a name." "What name?" "Stupid." "Well, just because I call you Mr. Prather, that does not make you the teacher. Just because he called you stupid doesn't make you stupid. Don't fall into their trap. When they say something silly, it is just to bother you. Outsmart them. Pay no attention. I know it's not easy, but it's smart."
- Give clear, precise instructions about everything. "The homework is due tomorrow. Any questions?" Change that to: "Your homework for tomorrow, Thursday, September 24, is to read the story I wrote for you about space travel, answer the five questions I gave you with two sentences for each answer and write a definition in your words to each of the 10 words we discussed that would be in the reading. When you arrive in class tomorrow, you will hand in your homework paper. Now, who can repeat what the homework is?"

SCHOOL THOUGHT 97

Managing the minute-to-minute details is demanding. Some ideas and methods:

- There is no perfect classroom management system. There are systems that work and those that do not, but the absence of a system is a guarantee of failure.
- "How old are you?" "Twelve." "How old are people who kick other people?" "I dunno. Maybe two." "Do you want to act like a two-year-old?"
- "When you break rules in class, you get in trouble. Do you want to get in trouble?" "No." "Good answer, so tell me, how can you avoid getting in trouble?"
- Going to lunch is not, "Walk quietly and wait for me in the cafeteria." It is "Line up in the hall by our classroom door. When you get to the stairway, stop." And other very specific clear, short-term instructions, plus your close and constant monitoring.
- Move throughout the classroom continuously. See everyone. Get near each student every few minutes. Students will realize that you could be anywhere at any time seeing anything anyone does.
- Observe your students in other classrooms. See what works there. See how they behave there. Ask: "I saw you behave perfectly in math. Explain that to me."

SCHOOL THOUGHT 98

Students watch teachers and other adults. Teach them while they are watching.

Use the power of your example. Be on time. Be prepared. Behave perfectly. Constantly display the behavior you require of students. This is true from the moment you arrive at school until the moment you leave. Also, you may be at a grocery store when a student sees you; that can give you a chance to set an example and to have some favorable interaction.

SCHOOL THOUGHT 99

When classroom situations occur that need swift, decisive disciplinary action, select your words carefully so no new problems are created. For example, "If you say one more word, I'm calling the principal" is not as good as "For each word you speak out of turn, you owe me one minute of silent lunch, one minute after school or one classroom chore I assign to you." Why dare them to make you call the principal? Don't back yourself into a corner—giving yourself some options can be helpful.

SCHOOL THOUGHT 100

When you chose teaching or when teaching chose you, it was more than a career decision. Sure, teaching is a job and teachers go to work, but, well, it's different from other jobs and other work. Teachers are part of the eternal human adventure, which, from the moment of creation to the end of time, compels people to know, to learn, to discover, to explore, to wonder, to think, to question, to make sense, to seek wisdom, to experience, to endure, to go from trial to error to correction, to confront reality and to live—to vibrantly and magnificently live.

To teach is to cause learning. A life of real, extreme teaching is a life of causing learning, of sharing learning, of significant interaction with students. It is a life that matters. To know that you are living a life that matters is a blessing and a joy. It is worth it. Extreme Teaching is intended to help make it worth even more.

NOTES

1. Henry David Thoreau, *Walden* (New York: Signet Classics, New American Library, 1960), 10.

2. Babbage, Keen J. *911: The School Administrator's Guide to Crisis Management* (Lanham, Md.: Scarecrow Press, 1996), 33–34.

Epilogue

"Good morning. Welcome back to school. I'm Mr. Prather, and I want you to know how glad and how thankful I am to be your teacher. Here's my first question for you: How many of you hate school? You can be honest. If you hate school, please tell me. Don't yell or scream or curse about it or about anything else, but if you hate school, please raise your hand."

A few silent and awkward moments passed until Jared raised his hand. Other students followed that example, until most of the class members had raised a hand.

"Let's figure out what those responses mean. First, is there any part of school that you do like?" The teacher was intentionally shifting to an opposite question. Students may have thought this class would be a time to complain about school, but now they had to see if they liked anything about school before they could complain.

Mr. Prather read the look on one student's face. "Hi. I bet you like seeing friends at school. True?" The student said, "Yeah, I like that, but that's about all I like. I just put up with the rest of it."

The discussion continued for several minutes. The students were really paying attention, were really listening and were really thinking. That set the stage for the next question. "Why is everyone paying attention so well if we are at school and most of you hate school?"

One student knew. "That's easy. We like to talk about what we don't like at school. You gave us a topic that is important to us. That's pretty cool."

Mr. Prather said a silent prayer of thanks and then told the students, "That is exactly right. You are experts on school, so you know what you think about it based on all of your years of experience. Now, here's an idea that may surprise you. I hate school. I love teaching and I really love being with students, but school can get in the way of what you and I really need to do. Bells, schedules, dull textbooks, meaningless homework, routine procedures, tests, conflicts and much more can take away from the adventures that school should really be about. I hate school when school gets in the way of you becoming incredible successes. I love school when we find ways to team up for you to become incredible successes. So, you and I have to find ways to make the successes happen. I'll show you how."

At that moment, each student was absolutely captivated by the teacher and by the class. Imagine, a teacher who would admit that he hates school but would then say that when everything worked well, he loves school. What was going on here?

It is called Extreme Teaching. This type of teaching is built upon these truths:

- Students learn every day—they may learn something wholesome, proper, beneficial and honorable or they may learn how to commit a crime, but young people in the childhood through teenage years learn continuously. The challenge is not to make students into people who can and do learn; they are already at that point. The challenge is to show students how and why to commit to learning at school.
- We know what works—think of the best teacher you ever had in any class or at a camp or at Sunday school or in your family. What did that teacher do that made such a difference? These teachers cared about you, they challenged you, they made learning interesting and worthwhile, they showed you how to apply what you learned, they were enthusiastic, they knew what they were teaching, they made learning real and they interacted with you in a genuine way. There are no secrets about great teaching. We know what works. No new research is needed. No new discoveries are needed. Just doing what works is needed.

Do you hate school? Do you hate textbooks and videos and mindless worksheets of meaningless busywork? Do you hate textbooks that have endless pages of dead information about irrelevant topics? OK, those phrases are rather are severe, but so are the dull, boring, empty experiences far too many students have to endure at far too many schools. Get real. Students make commitments to experiences that are real, that are meaningful, that are exciting, that are interesting, that apply to their real lives right now and that matter.

Extreme Teaching lives on the edge of academic adventures and of causing learning via a variety of methods. Extreme Teaching meshes with the realities that students are going to learn each day and that we know what great teachers do. Extreme Teaching gets out of the numbing mold and regressive routine of read the chapter, answer the questions, watch the video, fill out the worksheet and take a test on Friday. Those activities do not cause learning. Those activities are not teaching. A classroom clerk can supervise ordinary routines such as those.

Teachers are people who cause learning. Teaching means to cause learning. If the students did not learn, teaching did not happen. Schools and classrooms can have activities—making copies of worksheets, passing out the worksheets to students and grading the worksheets are activities—and seem to be busy places, but those schools and classrooms can also be places where the brains, the ideas, the ability, the imaginations and the energy of students get lost or numbed. Remember, no student will ever return to a school in the future and say to a teacher, "You know that worksheet you handed out in September of my junior year in high school? Wow, that really changed my life." Worksheets and the type of ordinary, dull, empty, meaningless classroom concepts and classroom activities they represent never touch lives. Extreme teachers touch lives. This book is about teaching methods and ideas and activities that can touch brains, minds, intellects, students, teachers and lives.

This book is about Extreme Teaching because students are eager to team up with extreme learning and because students are likely to reject—or just tolerate and go through the motions of—anything that is less than extreme in importance, in usefulness, in method of learning, in experience and in being real. Students stay ready to go to the extreme. This book is about how Extreme Teaching can create extremely beneficial classroom experiences for teachers and for students.

It is the author's hope that this book has ignited some extreme thinking, which will lead to Extreme Teaching, which will cause extreme learning by teachers and by students.

Index

Page numbers in italics refer to tables.

About the Author

Keen J. Babbage has taught social studies in grades 7–12 and has also taught education classes at the college and graduate levels. He has school administration experience with grades 6–12 and has executive experience with three large corporations.

Dr. Babbage has earned degrees from Centre College, Xavier University and the University of Kentucky. His doctoral work at Kentucky was during 1989–1993 as the Kentucky Education Reform Act was being developed, approved and initially implemented.

Dr. Babbage's dissertation dealt with the public policy process of implementing school-based decision making. In addition to this book, Dr. Babbage has written three others: *911: The School Administrator's Guide to Crisis Management*, *Meetings for School-Based Decision Making*, and *High-Impact Teaching: Overcoming Student Apathy*.

Dr. Babbage lives and works in Lexington, Kentucky.